"Opening and reading *Not My Child!* will be the most rewarding thing you could ever do for your children."

— Michael De Luca, parent, Rocky Point, NY

"I am excited about what *Not My Child!* means for children. If the author could teach us personally she would, but that's impractical and this book gives you time to read a little, put it down and digest it, then pick it up again and read on. Because it is full of information which a caring parent cannot afford to miss, every parent should finish it to the end for the full impact and benefit."

— Melody C. Gibson, parent, grandparent, and Executive Director/Co-Founder of Operation Lookout and The National Center for Missing Youth, Mukilteo, WA

"I found this book to be interesting, informative, well written, captivating, and compelling . . . I stayed awake until 2:00 a.m. to finish reading it!"

— Mary Cicero, parent, Austin, TX

"Great action portion - I can see myself teaching this to parents at evening sessions at my school and I can see me teaching it to kids in my counseling advisory classes."

— Carene Carlborn, parent and teacher, Milwaukee, WI

"Without question, parents who educate themselves and their children with the basic safety knowledge are empowered to act responsively rather than react helplessly to child abuse and abduction. The knowledge in *Not My Child!* should be in every parent's hands."

— Dr. George R. Jones, minister and former child abduction private investigator

"I have been soaking up all the information like a sponge! Finally, everything I should know in one place. My children thank you. I thank you."

— Susan Bodulow, parent, Petaluma, CA

Yello Dino Publishing is a child advocacy publishing organization that specializes in personal safety education through a variety of communication methods including books, printed material, music, video, computer games, and other electronic media. Yello Dino products are available wholesale to the trade, and at special discounts for bulk purchases for sales promotions, premiums, fund raising, or educational use. Special books, workbooks, book excerpts, songs, and other products can be created to fit specific needs. Yello Dino also offers other child security and identification products.

For details write or telephone:
Yello Dino Publishing
Post Office Box 33280
Austin, Texas 78764
(512) 288-4888

Yello Dino Publishing donates a portion of the proceeds of the sale of this book to organizations that help with missing, abducted and abused children.

NOT MY CHILD!

30 SIMPLE WAYS

To Help Prevent Your Child From Becoming
Lost, Missing, Abducted, or Abused

JAN WAGNER

"Not My Child!"
By Jan Wagner

Yello Dino Publishing
Post Office Box 33280
Austin, Texas 78764

Phone (512) 288-4888

Cover Design: Reuben King
Book Design: Reuben King & Barry Geller
Yello Dino Illustrations: Barry Geller

First Printing September, 1994
Library of Congress Catalog Card Number: 94-61259
ISBN 0–9641842–0–6

10 9 8 7 6 5 4 3 2 1

Table of Contents

Dedication

All my life I have been unable to forget the image in a photograph I saw when I was a teenager. It was of a mother holding her child. She seemed to be protecting her child. But from what, I wondered? This image touched my heart. During the media attention on missing children in the winter of 1993, the face of one mother struck me with the same force as that photograph. Two children had recently been abducted in her home town. The deep concern was obvious in her face and voice when she pleaded, "Tell me what I need to know to keep my children safe, and tell me now." This book is dedicated to that mother, and to all parents who simply want to know, "What can I do to help keep my children safe?"

Acknowledgements

With great pleasure I want to thank all the many people who have meant so much to me over the years, and who in their own way have helped contribute to the knowledge in this book and helped motivate me to write *Not My Child!*

It would be impossible to begin anywhere else than with my husband, Dennis. He has been my dearest friend since we first met in college. Ours has always been a very special relationship. He has been my greatest supporter in all aspects of my life. His contribution to this book is woven into each and every page. My parents, Ruth and Dick Thompson, my grandparents, Walter and Ethel Fravel, and my husband's parents, George and Kaye Wagner, showed us how much parents can care for their children. Their love, respect, and support over the years has been constant, and it has been a strength that would help any child reach for and achieve their dreams. My two children are the main reason that I faced my own denial response on the subject of missing and abused children, and went head-on into this difficult topic. Any child who has a working mother has to adjust to sharing her. My children have shown an incredible depth of loving support and understanding by sharing me so that other children would be helped; this has given me strength during the many long hours and late nights that have been necessary over the years.

My friend Karen Jonson's countless hours and tireless attention to research and detail has made this book possible. Her ability to help me express the knowledge I have gained over the years was invaluable. We spent many hours working side by side.

David Ham, Reuben King, and Barry Geller are special friends whose knowledge and expertise in advertising, communications, and design contributed greatly to shaping the information in this book. Additionally, David's original songs and musical contributions are truly a beautiful gift to children everywhere. Seth L. Goldstein brought an indispensable level of professional experience and knowledge on the subject of sexually abused children when he graciously agreed to join in and support our efforts in getting this important information directly to parents.

Special appreciation goes to all of the many SAFE-T-CHILD Directors who have helped me reach parents across the country with safety education and immediate response identification since 1987. The Directors' experience in the field has been fundamental in helping guide SAFE-T-CHILD in the direction most needed by parents. All of the Directors have generously given of themselves to help protect our children. I know their work has often been far from easy, but the testimony to our success is that together we have reached well over one million children already. Among the SAFE-T-CHILD Directors, I want to especially thank Major Calvin Jackson, George and Ann Jones, Ken and Paula Klett, Michael and Juliet De Luca, Julie Bradley, Guy Rossi, Norm Kronenberg, and Trish Charron-Holt for their invaluable commitment and knowledge.

Through the work of Janeen Brady I learned what a fabulous tool music can be for making a difficult subject like personal safety easy for children to learn. I would like to thank her for her pioneering work in safety music for children. I would also like to thank the media. Through the power of the media the topic of missing, abducted, and abused children has been brought to the attention of parents across the country and around the world. The media has taken a problem that has been growing quietly in our midst for generations and brought it into the light. Because the media is so powerful in our society in helping shed light on the reality of this subject, I have quoted liberally from several articles, television programs, and books. I would especially like to thank Oprah Winfrey for her bravery in publicly acknowledging her own childhood abuse, and for working to enact important changes for our children at the legislative level.

Over the years, I have talked with countless police officers, investigators, and many non-profit organizations. It would be impossible to give proper credit to everyone of them individually, but because of their love and concern for children, they have willingly shared their knowledge and experience with me. Their help has been indispensable and it is deeply appreciated. Most especially, the research conducted by Special Supervisory Agent Kenneth V. Lanning of the F.B.I.'s Behavior Science Unit has formed the basis of the knowledge used by investigators in recognizing and arresting the people who abduct and molest children. I also extend a hand of thanks to Melody Gibson, the Director and Co-Founder of Operation Lookout and the National Center for Missing Youth, for reading a pre-publication edition of this book and adding several valuable insights, which are based on her practical experience in finding missing children.

In addition, my sincerest respect goes to all the individuals at The National Center for Missing and Exploited Children and The Adam Walsh Foundation, founded by John Walsh (who alone has accomplished incredible feats), for the tremendous work they are doing to help the families of missing children and heighten the public's awareness of this extremely important topic.

Foreword

If there was ever a need to protect our children, there is an even greater need today. With each passing day, the media reports of missing, murdered, and molested children have placed this problem on the national agenda.

Compounding the problem are the shrinking budgets and misdirected priorities of public institutions, which have placed child assault prevention on the lowest level in years. This – and the fact that the child safety education programs which are in place are often only one-time events in a child's life – dictates that we as parents must take our children's protection into our own hands.

However, where do we start? A short 20 years ago children were given simplistic messages such as "look out for strangers with candy" and "if someone bothers you in the movie theater tell the usher." Today, we find that the lure of candy has has moved into trips to McDonald's, and that our children aren't even safe in our own homes let alone in public places such as movie theaters. In fact, children are kidnapped, molested, and murdered in virtually every place they play, pray, go to school, and live. In some cases, children have even been molested right in front of their parents without any adult realizing what was happening.

During the hundreds of child sexual abuse investigations I have worked on, one fact repeatedly came to the surface: children need personal safety tools to prevent abduction and molestation from happening in the first place. The best place for children to get that knowledge is in the home, from their parents. Parental involvement in children's safety education is even more important because children learn through repetition and reinforcement – two things which school programs can rarely afford. In your home, the lessons that you, as a parent, think are individually important and need emphasis can be repeated and reinforced with your child.

How then does a parent begin? Haphazard, non-specific, fear-producing discussions about safety issues will not give children the tools they can use to protect themselves from today's perils. Proper safety education requires a definite, planned, supportive framework which allows parents to educate their children in a non-threatening, proactive fashion.

The New York Police Department once published a prevention guide for children and parents that suggested parents "enlighten, not frighten" their children about personal safety. This is important, because we need children who, if ever confronted by a situation, have the ability to act logically, rather than be paralyzed by fear. Similarly, we do not want to create or instill in children a fear of the things they don't yet understand, such as their own or another person's sexuality. Through gradual and matter-of-fact discussions and lessons between parents and children, children will be empowered with knowledge and confidence.

Here is an example of one father's step in that direction: when the issue of missing children first entered the national spotlight and milk companies began publishing the photographs of missing children on milk cartons, a friend's 12-year-old read a milk carton one morning at breakfast and asked his dad, "What does 'abducted' mean?" His father, a seasoned police veteran of 20 plus years, simply asked, "What do you think it means?" The boy said that he though it meant that someone had taken the child. His father replied, "Yes, there are people who sometimes do bad things to children and you must be aware of it wherever you are." The boy said, "Oh" and that was the end of the conversation. The father had used neither fear nor hyperbole to answer his son's impromptu questions.

Clearly, it is our responsibility as parents to make sure our children comprehend the threat and have a plan to respond when confronted with the peril. When my wife and I asked our 10-year-old daughter what she would do if threatened by a dangerous person, she said that she would yell what her friend had told her to yell, "bloody murder." We used that opportunity to discuss with her how people would respond if she did yell that phrase, and we gave her some other options.

What a shame my colleague and I didn't have Jan Wagner's parent handbook, *Not My Child!: 30 Simple Ways to Help Prevent Your Child From Becoming Lost, Missing, Abducted, or Abused.* The book's simple and non-fearful guidelines to child security could have helped us take these important lessons even further with our children. The personal safety lessons contained in *Not My Child!* can be a lifesaver for your child. Jan has a dream to prevent "every parent's nightmare." To help make this dream a reality, she has spent countless hours researching, planning, and applying these child safety principles through The SAFE-T-CHILD Program, which has reached over one million children throughout the country.

The lessons and preventative tips described in *Not My Child!* are unique. What's more, they directly involve parents in preventing their children from becoming victims. The book's *30 Simple Ways* are a method of avoiding the haphazard and non-specific manner in which children are so often presented with safety lessons today.

The lessons afford parents the opportunity, through direct interaction with their children, to enlighten the spirit, body, and mind. This guidance will help permit parents to sleep more comfortably with the confidence and assurance that they have done nearly everything possible to help their children avoid and respond to any threat they might face. Used as directed, *Not My Child!* will definitely go a long way toward helping to prevent "every parent's nightmare."

Seth L. Goldstein, J.D.
Founder, The Child Abuse Forensic Institute
Author, *The Sexual Exploitation Of Children*
Napa, California, 1994

Preface

Everyone has a dream. But as we get older the reality of life seems to make our dreams too impossible to reach. So, we often bury them deep inside. From an early age, my dream centered around children. To me, the basis of a better world began with our children. I believed that only through them could true, positive changes be brought about in the world. But this vision lay dormant inside of me as my life progressed. Since my husband and I did not yet have children, my attention centered around our life together. I joined him in business and we began working side by side.

After years of hoping, I came to accept the fact that I was never going to be a mother. But how life likes to surprise us! After 11 years of marriage I was pregnant. Soon a beautiful baby girl was looking up at me and I was her mother. I said to my husband, "Forgive me if I just indulge myself in loving and raising her for a while." He smiled. As I immersed myself in motherhood, he joined me in the pleasure of watching and helping her grow. Life continued to play tricks and soon I was pregnant again. This time I had a beautiful little boy – born on his father's birthday. I thought I had died and gone to heaven; although being up a lot at night did tend to keep my feet on the ground.

Life has its ups and downs, and we were due for a down. The circumstances of our life changed dramatically when our children were two and four years old. A part of our life collapsed when a business venture, in which my husband was involved, failed. Due to the strain of this crisis his health gave way. My back was up against the wall. A mother's instinct to protect her family came charging to the surface. I needed to return to work and give him time to recover, but how could I work and still be a mother at home raising our children? I know it seems dramatic, but I could see us out on the streets, homeless and without food. Like all devastating experiences, if you look carefully, there is a golden lining. The dream of my younger days came back into my life. Why not combine providing for my family and helping children?

The seed sprouted. I excitedly began my research, and before I knew it I was offering Immediate Response Child I.D. Cards to parents in my community. I remember the first daycare I went to to take children's photographs and fingerprints for the I.D. cards. One little girl looked at me with a furrowed brow. As I carefully fixed her hair and wiped the jelly off of her face, I told her, "I'm a mommy too, just like your mommy. And she wants you to be safe; that's why she had me come see you, to help her keep you safe."

As I interacted with more and more parents, I kept hearing one question: "How can I *prevent* my children from ever becoming missing in the first place?" To help answer this question I continued researching deeper into this field. Since then, I have researched hundreds of parents' and children's personal experiences, case histories, clinical studies, the work of child abuse experts, and the work of police and investigators. It is not necessary for every parent to go through this much work to keep their children safer. This was not an easy task. Many times it was so heart-wrenching that I would have to stop and regain my composure. But I could see a ray of light in the midst of the darkness.

This led me to develop, with the invaluable assistance of many people, products and services that could really help prevent missing and abused children. The information blossomed into a small educational guidebook, filled with tips for keeping children safer, which we gave to every parent who participated in The SAFE-T-CHILD Program. Today, seven years later, the "Parent's Guide" has grown into this book. During this time, the research also led me to a powerful safety education tool: Music. As soon as we had the opportunity, we developed songs to help teach children the important safety concepts. Over the years we have also added several other security and identification products to our prevention and Immediate Response I.D. Program.

The SAFE-T-CHILD Program has grown in part on its own and in part through the dedication and love of many others, especially my husband and the SAFE-T-CHILD Directors. Through this child security organization, which I started in 1987, my dream is becoming a greater reality than I had ever hoped for. The SAFE-T-CHILD family of Directors has reached well over a million children already, and we are growing rapidly. The caring adults who have joined us come from around the world; each one is doing his or her part to weave a protective net for all our children. We are so thankful that you are taking the time to help your child, too. Together, we will create a safer world for all of our children.

Jan Wagner and the SAFE-T-CHILD staff and Directors
at the 1994 SAFE-T-CHILD Conference

Introduction

"How can a mother not help imagining that one day it might be her child's face on one of those posters?"
  – "Every Mother's Fear: Abduction," <u>Family Circle</u>

". . . *our modern world is dramatically different from that of any previous generation.* Social and family structures have drastically changed, as have the politics and economy of the world around us. All of this means that today's parents are faced with the challenges of managing new problems with their children that they may never have expected . . ."
  – Ava L. Siegler, Ph.D., <u>What Should I Tell the Kids?</u>

Who are these people from whom we have to protect our children? We don't know them, even though we may see them every day. Experts tell us they are around our children, but since parents are not trained to recognize them we can't protect ourselves or our children. This book is your handbook for a safer child.

Statistics tell us that each year there are about 115,000 attempted abductions of children (those were just the reported cases; thousands more incidents aren't reported). That means that thousands of children have used their "personal" safety skills to get away from people who meant to do them harm. The point is: We cannot always stop the people who harm children, but we can prepare our children to be among the ones, who – if they are ever approached – will have the knowledge to keep themselves safe.

Why did I write this book? To help children be safer in an unsafe world. These people who harm children need to be stopped. If there are no more victims they will be stopped. This book is a parent's handbook against an enemy that has no face, against an enemy who smiles sweetly at us and then commits crimes we cannot imagine. If we lived in a country at war, we would be alert to protecting our children. But because the enemy is not a soldier standing with a gun aimed at us, we are lulled into believing there is no one out to harm our children. This suits the perpetrators perfectly. They want us to leave our children unskilled in protecting themselves. Also, they like it when parents believe that this type of thing won't happen to their child. "Maybe the child down the street, but not mine," we desperately want to believe. But the next time you see someone else's child on the news, remember that is what the child abductors want you to think. Just look at the faces of the parents on the talk shows. They never thought it would happen to their children either. Over and over again they say, "If I'd just taught my child that she had the right to say 'no,' or if I'd taught him to yell and scream if anyone tried to grab him . . . maybe the outcome would have been different."

> "'. . . each year,' added [John] Walsh, 'there are about three hundred unsolved nobody-knows-what-happened-to-them long-term missing kids. Some say three hundred kids a year isn't much. I say if there's three hundred police or three hundred journalists or three hundred anchormen missing a year, it would be a big problem. And I say this: If it was your kid, one of those three hundred, it would be a big problem.'"
> – Paulette Cooper and Paul Noble, <u>Reward</u>

When discussing the issue of missing children, the 150 to 300 reported cases of children taken long-term by strangers each year, however, are just the tip of the iceberg.

Many more children are abducted short-term and returned home (3,200 to 4,600*), are kidnapped by non-custodial parents (354,100), are runaways (450,700), are throwaways (127,100), or are injured or missing for some other reason (438,200). The U.S. Justice Department estimates that these six categories total nearly 1.4 million children. There are also the uncountable cases of sexual abuse of children – a temporary form of abduction.

This book is not just about the "tip of the iceberg." The knowledge and action steps presented here cross over into many areas where parents need accurate information to help keep their children safer. The intention of this book is to give parents a balanced perspective of a child's personal security in the 1990's, and to provide a positive, supportive framework for implementing that knowledge into every parents' role as protector of their children.

In a society that moves so fast that we live our lives in a reactive mode, prevention is rarely addressed. The media gives tremendous air time to sensational stories about abducted and abused children, but the amount of time actually given to useful and real *preventative* knowledge seems minuscule by comparison. Sensationalism brings high ratings. Prevention doesn't. One show, advertised as providing safety knowledge to parents, actually dedicated only a few minutes to prevention. The rest of the show focused on family members of abducted children and their sorrow.

Even some friends of mine who have watched as SAFE-T-CHILD developed over the years, still never really felt this topic applied to their children. One friend in particular is a great mother of two lovely children. She knew I was writing this book and she agreed to read the first rough draft. The next day she came to see me and said,

---

*All figures are from a report published by the U.S. Department of Justice (nationwide estimates extrapolated for 1988).

"I really didn't want to hear what you have been trying to tell me all these years. But after reading your book I am starting tonight and going over one safety lesson with my children each night until we've reviewed all 30 Simple Ways. Thank you," she said as she hugged me. I was so pleased that this book made it easier for her to accept this important area of parenting. Also, it provided her with a simple way to teach personal safety to her children - *just* the thing many parents have been lacking. I know if I could reach her, I can reach you.

Through the knowledge in this book I am hoping that parents will get mad, then get serious about teaching their children personal safety. I'm also hoping that no parent will ever again have to say, "If I'd only known . . ." I'd prefer that parents everywhere join me in my refrain: "Not My Child!"

Special Note

Child Abuse Is A Temporary Form of Abduction

While writing about keeping children safe from ever becoming lost, missing or abducted, it is nearly impossible not to cross over into the area of sexual abuse. For one thing, abductors (whether adults or teenagers) almost always kidnap children for the purpose of sexually abusing them. For another, any form of sexual abuse, whether by a family member or non-family member, is really a form of temporary abduction.

This temporary abduction can begin with a stranger pulling the child into an alley or luring him into a vehicle. Or it can begin with a family member or friend taking the child into a bedroom. In every case, during the abuse the child is isolated from adults who can help them. The child is essentially a prisoner until the adult decides the encounter is over.

When I learned that research studies show that from 10 percent to 40 percent of boys and girls under the age of 18 will experience some form of sexual abuse, I wished that I could turn away from this painful topic. But through further research I came to the conclusion that it would be a disservice to parents and their children to allow the veil of ignorance surrounding the sexual abuse of children to continue. After all, it is because of this silence that sexual abuse takes place generation after generation.

So, rather than ignore the issue of sexual abuse, I integrated it into this book. One of the most significant aspects of the personal safety rules for children is that they apply to the prevention of long-term abduction as well as to the prevention of the temporary form of abduction known as sexual abuse.

CHILD SECURITY IN THE 1990'S

The Non-Fearful Approach

"'Telling a child that some bad people exist is very different from telling him that the world is a bad place, full of bad people' [says author Grace Heehinger]."
  – "Missing Children," <u>American Baby</u>

"All parents may sometimes be reluctant to teach their young ones about strangers, concerned that the information will make the kids fearful. But remember that information empowers children. 'What terrifies a child is ignorance,' says John Walsh, founder of the Adam Walsh Child Resource Center . . . 'You owe it to your child to give him appropriate, intelligent information,' he asserts. And you owe it to yourself, for your own peace of mind."
  – "Careful, Not Fearful," <u>Sesame Street Parents' Guide</u>

As the founder of SAFE-T-CHILD, I have found that fear regarding children's personal safety is a real concern among parents. And not just the fear of losing a child, but the fear of even discussing this topic with their children. Parents do not want to scare their children. Even when I have approached friends with safety knowledge, a few have said, "You're not going to scare my children are you?" My response is, "They are probably already scared." And even the most protective parents and guardians can't protect their children from the information that comes at them over television and in school.

Children are egocentric. They think that the things

they hear about will happen to them. During the extensive media attention on 12-year-old Polly Klaas's abduction and murder in Petaluma, California, in late 1993, a <u>Time</u> magazine article reported that, "The number one topic among third-graders was abduction." With all of the media attention focusing on the sensationalism of kidnapping and abuse, very little attention was given to proactive solutions. No wonder children often feel afraid and helpless. Also, children become afraid when they sense that their parents are afraid.

My response to parents who are worried about scaring their children is: Why should it be scary to teach kids how to stay safe, to teach them to say "no" if they don't like being touched in a certain way, to run or yell if they feel threatened, and to always ask for their parent's permission before going anywhere?

Taking the non-fearful approach to child safety reminds me of a story I once read in *Reader's Digest* about a little girl who asked her father about a troubling issue of our modern times. The father, who was on his way to work, told his daughter he would answer her question, but first he wanted her to carry his briefcase to his car. She agreed. But as she attempted to pick up the briefcase she found that it was too heavy. She told her father that she couldn't lift it. He knelt down and explained to her that some things in the world are like his briefcase, too heavy for her to carry right now. When she was a little older she would be able to pick up his briefcase, and when she was a little older he could answer her question, because then she'd be able to handle it. Sharing safety information with our children is similar: you tell your children only as much as they can handle for their particular age. For example, you cannot explain to a three-year-old the concepts of how some people use "lines" to lure children away (parents must take the responsibility to watch children who are three or younger at all times). But by the time a child is four you can start introducing the

4

concept of "tricky people" and describe some of the simple lines they use. Then you can build on this knowledge as the child grows up.

As parents it is our job to educate our children about topics that are important to their welfare. However, when we have to share knowledge about scary issues we do not have to make the information fearful. My concept of safety education does not involve telling our children that there is a man on every street corner waiting to steal them. And just as we do not describe the ramifications of being hit by a car when we tell children to look both ways before crossing the street, similarly, we do not have to scare them about personal safety. I prefer presenting safety education in a non-fearful, empowering format.

I've seen first-hand the benefit of safety education with my own children and their friends. One night my son and daughter and a couple of their friends (ages 8 to 14) were together. I asked them to watch two videos. First, I showed them an evening news report on the abduction and subsequent murder of a child. Their feelings of fear and helplessness filled the room. Could this happen to them? They all felt that yes, it could.

I put in the second video. This was an educational program that described how children can protect themselves from ever being abducted. While we watched the program, each child's expression changed from fear to confidence. We discussed the information and how they personally would respond in a variety of situations. As I praised their correct answers and guided them to a clearer understanding of what they can do to stay safe, I could literally feel them becoming stronger and more confident. This was such a dramatic example of the power of non-fearful education for me. There are no two ways about it, knowledge empowers children. If we give children the right knowledge and training, they will generally be able to pull themselves out of a crisis.

The "30 Simple Ways" presented in this book are valuable tools for parents. Along with these safety lessons, there is an educational tool that charms children and makes it possible for them to understand difficult concepts. It is music. The SAFE-T-CHILD Program has been offering safety education through music for many years. Music is powerful, fun, non-threatening, and easy for children to remember. Parents are always surprised when they find that their children want to play and sing the safety songs over and over again. Countless parents have expressed their joy – and relief – with the music's success. Without question, music gives parents an invaluable aid in this challenging area of parenting. Teaching through music is therefore one of the cornerstones of "the non-fearful approach."

The success of non-fearful safety education will be realized when your children feel strong and confident as they grow up safer in an unsafe world. How wonderful for parents to have this peace of mind!

Getting Through
The Denial Response

"The country's in denial. Kidnapping by strangers is a terrifying thing."
> – David Collins (of the Kevin Collins Foundation, whose son Kevin was kidnapped in 1984), "Father Dedicates His Life to Searching for Missing Kids," CNN's *Prime News*

"To bury your head in the sand and say my child could not be victimized, in light of all the things that have happened in this country and what continues to happen, is doing your child a disservice. It's tough stuff. But you've got to remember your child is the potential victim. You won't be the victim."
> – John Walsh, "How to Raise a Street Smart Kid," *HBO*

"I think that it can happen anywhere you have the offender – and they're everywhere."
> – Bowling Green Police Lt., "Kids and Strangers," WKRC-TV 12, Cincinnati

Denial surrounding the topic of child abduction and abuse is rampant. It takes many forms. For example, some people like to remind us that, "Only 300 children a year are taken by strangers." Then there are the adults who see children hanging around the house of a man down the street day after day, but ignore their gut feeling that something isn't right.

Admittedly, it is easy to understand why parents want to believe that if they don't think about it, it will go away and never happen to them. And why so many others hope, wish, and pray that this will never happen to their children. As mentioned previously, sometimes I too turn away from the facts and say, "This is just too much for me to think about right now." But how can a parent honestly ignore this topic? How can we deny that it exists when the facts tell us that it is all too real?

While offering child security education over the years, I have sometimes had to resort to the frightening facts to get parents' attention. I am not trying to scare them. I am trying to wake them up. Fear just happens to be one of the best motivators. And if the facts are the only thing that will wake parents up, then I will call on the facts every time. Here are some common forms of parental denial, along with a "real-world" perspective:

My children are too young. "Child molesters never think that your kids are too young." (Major Calvin Jackson (USAF, Ret.), SAFE-T-CHILD Director and former child abuse investigator)

It won't happen in my small town. Listen to the words of one convicted child molester: "I went through her window. My plan was just to do it while they were asleep and they'd never know about it. I committed the perfect crimes . . . Sure you like to think of small towns as being safe. Small towns [are] easy." (Convicted child abductor, NBC's *Now*)

It only occurs in the inner city. "'One of the things about this case is that we are an ordinary middle-class family, not rich, not poor. We weren't living in the 'wrong part of town.' My husband and I both have good professions, and we were two immigrants who made good. We always put our kids first. We taught Allison to be careful, and she was a child who obeyed the rules. If this can happen to us, it can happen to anybody.'" (Mother of 11-year-old girl abducted and murdered by a man who wanted to "photograph" her, <u>Reward</u>, Paulette Cooper and Paul Noble)

Clearly, burying your head in the sand will not change the reality. Unfortunately, it often takes highly publicized abductions to break through many parents' denial. For example, I saw so many parents and children frightened by Polly Klaas's abduction and subsequent murder in late 1993. That abduction occurred in a small town and Polly was taken out of her own home, from her own bedroom with her mother asleep just down the hall. This incident is among the handful in our history that truly awakens parents to the possibility that this could happen to their children. This abduction, in particular, shattered many parents concept of what they must do to keep their children safe. I felt the impact immediately. Following that incident, more parents than ever participated in our child security program.

I would prefer if parents took a proactive approach instead of a reactive approach to keeping their children safe. If abduction or molestation occurs it is a violation of a child's life that can never be fully repaired. I would rather that parents and children are a little scared and deal with this issue, than risk letting another child get hurt deeply for the rest of his or her life.

I believe that when parents grasp the true need for safety education they will not avoid the responsibility. Parents often deny tough subjects because they feel, deep down, that they can't do anything to change the problem. Denial is a form of fear, and fear is removed by knowledge. This book will give you the knowledge as well as the specific action steps you need to remove the fear and be proactive about your children's safety – and more easily and effectively than you could imagine. With the correct knowledge, this is one of the few areas of parenting where you can accomplish so much. And it is one of the areas of parenting, which with only a little time, you can make such an important difference in how a child's life turns out.

9

Parents' Responsibility

". . . parents have the primary responsibility for keeping their children safe . . ."
  – "Missing Children: The Ultimate Nightmare," <u>Parents</u>

"You need to understand that you can reduce the odds. You can empower your children to stay safe. You can't make them absolutely safe, but you can make them safer."
  – Rosie Gordon's father (10-year-old Rosie was abducted and murdered), "How to be Safe in America," ABC News' *PrimeTime Live*

Just as parents take the responsibility to teach their children about good hygiene, proper nutrition, and moral behavior, they must take the responsibility to teach children about how to keep themselves safe. Why is it parents' responsibility to educate their children about personal safety? One main reason: nobody else knows or loves your children as you do.

Some parents count on schools or community organizations to educate their children about safety education. But this is not enough. As a parent, how do you know that your child has truly learned all of the important safety rules? What if he or she were sick one day and missed an important lesson? Or, in a class of 20 children, is there time to ask every child his response and then wait to see if some other thoughts bubble up? Also, the safety classes in schools are usually limited to a specific day or week when, in fact, to be truly effective safety education must be ongoing.

Clearly, parents must be the primary source for educating and reinforcing safety knowledge with their children. Because parents know their children better than anyone else, they are the only ones who can ensure that their children truly comprehend what they have learned. Moreover, the most natural environment for reinforcing children's knowledge as they grow is in the parent-child relationship, not a classroom environment.

The advantages of parents educating their children about personal safety include the following:

Review and repeat. Repetition is important with children because they have short memories. When you work with them, you have the opportunity to regularly review the information you teach them and the information they may have learned in school. And you can test them through role-playing and what-if games to make sure they fully understand how to keep themselves safe. Also, when you instruct them, your children receive the added value of one-on-one learning. This can help strengthen your parent-child bond.

Make the information age-appropriate. You can make sure the information they receive is appropriate for their age. Children require different safety rules and different levels of information depending on their age. As a parent you have the unique advantage of being able to update their safety knowledge as they mature. For example, as previously mentioned, you cannot expect a three-year-old to understand the concept of strangers, so you must make sure they know not to run away from you in a public place. By four, they can begin to understand who a stranger is and how to be more cautious around people they do not know.

Tailor information. You can tailor the information to match your child's unique personality, and you can modify the information to fit your child's natural strengths and

11

weaknesses. For example, some children are outgoing and so will not flinch when you tell them to say "no" to an adult if they feel threatened or tricked. Another child may be shy and, therefore, need more encouragement to assert himself around adults. A third child will be very compassionate and friendly and have a more difficult time not talking to people she does not know. A fourth child might be intrigued and, therefore, easily drawn in by the influence of others.

Create an emergency plan with your family members. Together, you and your children can create a plan for your family, before an emergency arises, that includes the rules that your family members follow to stay safe. For example, you can decide together who can pick up the children from school in case of a family emergency, where exactly the children would run to if they were scared while walking home, and what to say to a caller when you are not at home. One of the SAFE-T-CHILD Directors, Trish Charron-Holt, suggested that parents create an "agreement" with their child, much like the contract suggested by Mothers Against Drunk Drivers (MADD). In the agreement, you and your child can agree on actions that he or she will take in a variety of situations.

Parents can only adequately fulfill their responsibility of educating their children about safety when they themselves are educated. The Action Steps in this book will provide parents with the knowledge they need to bring safety education into the natural course of raising their children.

Who Are The "Bad Guys?"

"They called him the Big Brother."

"I trusted him."

"His friends say he loved children. Police say he hunted them."
> – Comments about a convicted child killer, "Child Hunter," CBS's *48 Hours*

"I don't know why, I just have to do this every so often. It helps to relieve the tension."
> – Comment by a man after he killed a young girl, FOX's *America's Most Wanted*

"There is no (psychological) profile" to help parents identify a molester.
> – Ian Russ, Ph.D., ABC's *The Home Show*

With dismay in their voices, parents often ask, "Who would do this type of thing?" If only there was an easy answer. Unfortunately, there is not. In this section, I have tried to give parents useful information without going into the deeply disturbing nature of these people. My hope is that from this information more abductors and molesters will be recognized and stopped sooner.

The problem of "who are the bad guys" starts with one fundamental fact: we cannot pick them out from the people who live and work within our everyday lives. According to author Seth L. Goldstein in *The Sexual Molestation of Children*, "Not all child molesters are the same. Not all molesters are pedophiles. Not all child molesters are passive, non-aggressive people. Child molesters come in all shapes, sizes, races, sexes, and ages and are motivated by a wide variety of influences. There is no single investigative or interview technique to deal with all of them." One psychologist who worked with convicted child molesters says that among the group in one therapy session was a doctor, a teacher, a lawyer, and only one person who anyone could describe as the "dirty old man."

One of the reasons that we cannot pick them out is that they work hard at being viewed as "normal" so that their behavior will not be suspected. To let you know how deceptive some of these people are, here are a few of the kinds of descriptions of convicted child abductors and molesters from the people who knew them that you might hear:

"He was a good boy, he liked to help people. He went to preachers' school, he was a gentleman, intelligent, quiet, a good Samaritan."

"He was a good kid, a favorite with children. He was president of the local Kiwanis Club."

"He bought the kids bicycles and toys, and he was so helpful."

Who would guess that these types of people abduct, molest, even kill, children? No one, and that's the problem. But while we cannot identify them, there are some similarities in profile, including these:

• They often lack social competence with adults.

• They usually seek legitimate access to children through jobs and volunteer work.

• They spend unusual amounts of time with children.

• They, in many cases, were abused children. Because they are hurt from abuse and didn't receive treatment, they rarely acknowledge the hurt they inflict on children.

• They seem to have two sides to their personalities.

14

• Normally they are not correctable; studies have shown that people who are attracted to children cannot be changed. It is important to remember that if you know someone who was convicted of child molestation, you should not be lulled into thinking it won't happen again.

Here are a few statistics that I, personally, find shocking (this information was compiled by Kenneth V. Lanning, Supervisory Special Agent with the F.B.I.'s Behavioral Science Unit). In his study of 561 sex offenders, Dr. Gene Abel found pedophiles who targeted young boys outside the home committed the greatest number of crimes with an average of 281.7 acts with an average of 150.2 partners. Molesters who targeted girls within the family committed an average of 81.3 acts with an average of 1.8 partners. He also found that 23.3 percent of the 561 subjects offended against both family and non-family targets. Hard to believe, isn't it? Clearly, this is not a small problem. We don't know who they are. We don't know how many are out there. What we do know is that they live and work in our communities.

But where do these people come from? When we look around us, the signs are there. One is the breakdown of the family unit. Our society has created an environment where children can be raised into dangerous adults. The security and strength of a strong family unit that provides the loving environment for raising children is gone. We live in a mobile society. The members of the family are rarely found in the same town, let alone the same state. Mothers have joined the work force in increasing numbers. This has been brought about by the economic pressures requiring two parents to work to meet basic living needs. Now, over 60 percent of mothers work due to necessity and another 20 percent choose to work. This places additional strain on the collapsing family unit.

There is another growing dilemma: single parenting. Over 50 percent of households are run by single parents, who can't be everywhere at once. How can one person realistically provide all the needs of a child that were once handled by grandparents, aunts, uncles, husbands, wives, cousins, and siblings? It is simply impossible. When you take a hard look at our society, is it really any surprise that our children are so vulnerable to the friendship offered by a child molester? The disintegration and problems of the family is recounted over and over again in our media. Here are just a few quotes:

> "In her years as a prosecutor, [Attorney General, Janet] Reno saw first hand the link between a miserable child and a vicious adult."
> –"Truth, Justice and the Reno Way," <u>Time</u>

> "'The current system has already pulled the family apart . . . Nothing could be more harmful than that.'"
> – (Robert Rector, a senior policy analyst with the Heritage Foundation), "The Vicious Cycle," <u>Time</u>

> "'I firmly believe that the biggest danger to us is the disintegration of the American family.'"
> -(George Bush, former US President), "The Grandfather in Chief," <u>Time</u>

If you want to build a building, the foundation is critical. If it is weak, the whole building will suffer. If it is too weak, it will collapse. We ask, "Who are these people?" They are the ones who could not survive a weak foundation and they have "collapsed." These people were once children. They were victims. Now many of our children will become their victims. Research shows that child abductors and molesters themselves were often molested as children. In their attempt to fulfill distorted needs they, as adults, draw in children – just as they were drawn in. We must realize that there are thousands of hurting children who might grow up and continue the cycle. Among the many

16

studies conducted on the sexual abuse of children, it has been found that, depending on the focus of the research, 10 percent to 40 percent of all children today will encounter some form of molestation before they are 18 years old. (These statistics do not include the activities of children who are naturally curious about their bodies.) This problem is not limited to the inner cities, to one economic class, or to one race. There are, in fact, no limitations on where and when child abuse can occur. This problem has existed for generations and has been dealt with poorly. It can no longer be swept under the carpet.

Another important fact for parents to know is that many abductors and most molesters are actually seeking love and affection, but in a distorted way. Because gaining love through children requires an indirect approach, abusers have developed "patterns" for entangling children. One of these approaches is to "stalk" a child over a few hours, days, or months. Molesters may even take a year to build the relationship before they actually begin the physical abuse. They even have a name for this approach – they call it "grooming" the child. Clearly, the abuser is often far from a stranger by the time the actual abuse takes place. Here are the chilling words of one child molester from the HBO video, "How to Raise a Street Smart Kid":

"It's this sixth sense most molesters have that they know the child won't put up much resistance. I gave them this feeling. I gave them the feeling of affection, of belonging, of being wanted. And it was like spinning a spider web and before you know it, they're caught . . . Most of my victims were easy targets. If you're into it really, and you want to pick up kids off the streets, you pick one that's always alone. And the look on their faces. You can tell the look on their faces. That sad puppy-dog-eyed look . . . I'll do this for you, I'll take you somewhere if you do something for me. Most cases they trusted me; 80 percent of the time my victims would do whatever I asked them to do."

Further, in extensive research conducted by Supervisory Special Agent Kenneth V. Lanning of the F.B.I.'s Behavioral Science Unit, child abductors have been shown to fall into five general categories and child molesters into two general categories. They are the following:

Child Abductors:

1. Non-traditional. These include women who kidnap babies from hospitals. Most often they steal the babies to fill an emotional need, to preserve a relationship with a man, or fulfill a need to mother if they cannot have children.

2. Profit. This group steals children because they know the child has a monetary value, usually in an underground network.

3. Ransom. Here the kidnappers take the child to sell back to its parents.

4. Sexual. These are the abductors who take a child to have sex. Once their goal is accomplished they either keep, return (the majority), discard, or kill the child.

5. Child killer. This group takes children for the primary motivation of killing them. They may also have sex with them, but not necessarily.

6. Miscellaneous criminal. This is a catch-all category to include all other forms of child abduction, for example if a bank robber takes a child as a hostage.

Child Molesters:

1. Situational. Situational abusers are not specifically attracted to children, but take advantage of an opportunity to have sex with a child due to either some regression, a lack of morals, a desire to "try anything," or mental deficiencies.

18

2. Preferential (pedophile). Pedophiles interact with children primarily for sexual gratification; in fact, many are addicted to children. Pedophilia is a way of life for this group, some even have newsletters to communicate with each other. They spend much of their time trying to convince themselves that they are giving love to and receiving love from children. They usually seduce children with attention, affection, and gifts.

Through all of this appalling information on the people who hurt children, we must keep a healthy, balanced perspective. We have to remember that the majority of the people in the world do not abuse children. It will not do us or our children any good to blow out of proportion the natural – and harmless – affectionate interactions between children and adults. We simply need the knowledge and the awareness to spot truly inappropriate behavior and action. Parents and children must understand this or the natural loving interactions of family members and friends with our children will be unnecessarily harmed. Loving physical interaction is crucial for children. After all, who couldn't use a big hug!

Stranger Danger:
Myth and Reality

"'It isn't strangers [we have to fear],' Sutherland says, 'it's us. If you keep drilling 'beware of strangers,' you're missing 90 percent of what happens to kids. Ninety percent of what happens is done by non-strangers–parents, stepparents, extended family, neighbors, friends . . . people the kids know.'"

> – "Missing Children," <u>American Baby</u> (Charles Sutherland, publisher of <u>The Missing Persons Report</u>, Search, Inc.)

"Many unanswered questions still bother Mrs. Przybylak [Mandy's mother]. 'Was Mandy taken from our house or did she go into someone's truck earlier? I believe she wouldn't have gone with a stranger. If somebody tried to make Mandy do what she didn't want, she would scream or run like hell. But she knew the person she went off with,' she speculates."

> – "Mysteries for a Mother," <u>Reward</u>, Paulette Cooper and Paul Noble

I am thankful that the majority of adults who work with children are good, caring professionals. Over the years I have met and talked to many people who have gained my respect because of their dedication to helping children. These caring adults have dedicated their lives to protecting, recovering, and helping to heal children who were not able to protect themselves. One of these people is a psychologist who specializes in child abuse at the National Institute of Mental Health in Maryland. Jim Breiling's years of work in

20

this area have given him clear insight into the issue of child abuse. When we asked him what information would be the most valuable to help parents keep their children safe from abuse, his answer was, "Tell parents to check out their friends and family members first." This may not be what we all would like to hear.

Of course, through the media, we always hear about and fear most the dramatic cases of *stranger* abduction and molestation. To protect their children, parents buy personal alarms, enroll their children in self-defense courses, and set up teams of parents to walk children home from school. But the fact remains: the circle of adults and caregivers around a child is the first ring that needs to be secure. The statistics vary from 70 percent to 90 percent, but every source says the same thing – children are sexually abused by people the child's family knows. Often it is a family member or close family friend. Sometimes it is someone the child or family sees in the regular course of their lives, such as a worker at the school, a checkout clerk at the neighborhood grocery store, or a person who lives down the street. That is why, despite media reports that often focus on stranger danger, parents need to know that strangers are not the most probable source of harm to their children.

Regarding sexual abuse within families, Major Calvin Jackson (USAF, Ret.), a leading forensic expert, former child abuse investigator in the U.S. military, and now a SAFE-T-CHILD Director, found that abuse is woven throughout the entire structure of a family. The abuse often has deep roots, and to try and cut those roots often means breaking apart the family – an option often too difficult for the family members to face. As such, families may have great difficulty dealing with the abuse at all. In many of Major Jackson's cases, the child would talk in confidence to a close friend, then that friend would tell his parents, and those parents would contact officials. If the case reached the courts, a key witness in the family often backed out before the trial date, usually to avoid further conflict within the family. Then Major Jackson's hands were tied. Tragically, he had no avenue for helping the children.

Convicted abusers are, perhaps, our best source of advice on this issue. They say that parents are too quick to trust people with their children. One man said, "The parents let me baby-sit their children after knowing me for only one week. They felt that I was safe because I worked with children in my profession."

To understand how their minds work, let's take a simple example. If you really want to learn how to play golf, you spend time at the golf course. You put yourself in the circumstances to get what you want. Child abductors and molesters do just that. In fact, studies show that child molesters will choose jobs or volunteer activities that put them in direct contact with children, such as teachers, coaches, and troop leaders. Also, it is not uncommon for child molesters who were discovered abusing children in one state to simply move to another state, get another job working with children, and start all over again. An example of this occurred in Plano, Texas. During the investigation of an abduction of a young girl at a soccer field, officials conducted background checks on the soccer coaches and found that the head of the soccer league was a convicted child molester from another state. (Due to specific circumstances, he was not a suspect in this case. Interestingly, no one had checked him out, either.) The man who did abduct and kill the seven-year-old was a convicted child molester out on parole. Further investigation showed that he had been forced to move from his previous home town because of incidents of abuse that occurred there.

In one case of child abuse, the parents immediately befriended their son's new scout leader, and invited him to dinner. The mother of the abused child says, "He brought four children with him that I thought were his. Later I found out that he was abusing them, as well . . . They want you to feel secure with them. They draw you in."

One point to consider: if a person likes to be with your child more than you do there is probably something wrong. Of course! Who loves your child more than you? Here are a few points parents can use as a guideline to observing adult's behavior around their children:

• Find out why an adult wants to spend unsupervised time with your child.

• Find out what attraction there is for your child to spend a lot of time at an adult's home.

• Be watchful of adults who shower your children with gifts or invite them on outings.

• Watch out for adults who use games that are really lures and tricks that will become a means to entrap a child into a physical relationship. An adult may use a few simple toys or games, or he might go to the extreme and create his home into a virtual playland for children.

• No one does something for nothing; if they look too good to be true, they just might be.

• Ask for several references, including job and volunteer work, from adults in positions such as troop leaders and follow up with phone calls to the references. When talking to the references be sure to ask how long they have known the person who will be spending time with your child. If they are new to your town, find out why they left their previous home. Don't take their word for it, do the best you can to talk to a variety of references.

• Make sure your child knows that they should tell you if any adult touches them in any way that doesn't feel right.

When the myth of "Stranger Danger" is realized, parents will be able to offer their children a more safe and secure environment in which to grow up.

Education is the
First Safety Rule

"The best defense against abduction and the general fear surrounding the subject is education. If we can give children accurate guidelines appropriate to their ages and teach them to be on the lookout for certain kinds of individuals and situations, we can help them to become careful and confident, rather than overly cautious and fearful, as they grow up in a world that is less than perfect."
   – "Every Mother's Fear: Abduction," Family Circle

"'The real lesson to be learned from cases like Cassidy Senter's and Polly Klaas's,' advocates say, 'is how valuable awareness and education can be. No neighborhood watch or electronic device can replace solid safety rules and emergency strategies for children.'"
   – "Awareness, Education Help Fight Abduction," Austin American-Statesman

"Education is a child's best self-defense because 75% of self-defense is mental. Only 20% is physical and 5% is luck. Therefore, there is absolutely no excuse for any child to be without the right personal safety and security knowledge."
   – Sensei David Ham, Member of Aikikai Foundation, Hombu Dojo, Tokyo, Japan

Safety education is an ongoing part of parenting. The sooner the process begins the easier it is to keep the dialogue open as your children grow. My own children certainly receive ongoing information about keeping themselves safe, so I've seen first hand the value it has brought to their lives. While educating your children about personal safety, don't try to cover everything in one "learning" session or even in a few nights. Instead, using small, easy steps, make it a part of their whole life. Modify and expand on the safety concepts to make them appropriate to their age – so that they, in effect, grow up with safety knowledge.

Music, role-playing, and teaching by example are among the important steps in educating your children to stay safer. Here is how they can help.

Music: The fun way to learn safety rules

Music is a fabulous tool for teaching children safety tips. But from what I've observed, its value has been largely underestimated. For years, we have seen the powerful results of offering safety education music for children. It has been popular and effective for four reasons:

1. Music is fun,

2. Music is easy and doesn't require a lot of time,

3. Music is a non-fearful way to instruct children about a serious topic, and

4. Children remember concepts when they learn them through music. In fact, studies show that they retain almost 90 percent of what they hear and sing as opposed to only about 10 percent of what they are told. Music is also great for reinforcing information, because children will play the songs over and over again. To understand the power of music, think about how you can recall the lyrics to songs that you heard years ago.

For years we have received grateful comments from parents who have used safety music to help them educate their children about personal safety. Their words express their feelings better than I can:

> "Recently, Tom's son was having a difficult time sleeping at night, and we had tried everything we could think of to make him less scared. In a frantic moment, I reached over for the safety tape we purchased from you, and turned it on for him. He was asleep in 15 minutes! When we talked to him the next day, he said that the tape made him feel 'safe.'"
>
> – Sue Arrigo, mother, Indiana

> "The children really enjoy the music, and they ask us to play the tape all the time, as it has quickly become their favorite."
>
> – Richard L. Bowen, M.D., father, Florida

> "My daughter could not remember our area code no matter how hard I tried until I played the music for her. After listening to the telephone song a few times, she not only learned her telephone number, but she remembered it."
>
> – Robyn Gross, mother and SAFE-T-CHILD Director, Maryland

Because music is such an easy, fun, and effective way for children to learn safety rules, we have been involved in creating new music to broaden and further reinforce the important safety concepts. This new safety education music, published by Yello Dino, is based on the latest research on how children can keep themselves safe. For example, some of the songs on the *Can't Fool Me!* album are: "Tricky People," which teaches children how to identify some of the "lures" adults use to abduct children; "My Body's Mine" teaches children that they are in control of their bodies and can set limits for physical affection; and "Help Me Operator" teaches children how to remember their telephone number and when to call emergency numbers for help. (Full song lyrics and a commentary on each song in the *Can't Fool Me!* album can be found in Appendix D.) These powerful messages will help children stay safe and free.

Role-Playing

Just as children have an easier time learning safety concepts through music, they also have an easier time learning things that *they* say or do, as compared to what they see and hear. That is why "what-if" games and role-playing are such valuable teaching methods. Because they are interactive, these games instill the safety skills into children's bodies and minds. Also, through role-playing, parents can find children's weak spots and work on them, and they can regularly reinforce the safety rules with their children. Remember, it is much better to play out a potentially scary situation with a child than to have them experience it unprepared.

In the "what if" game format, children's fears often bubble to the surface. They must be in an environment where they can express their feelings or fears. Your own parent-child relationship is the most important, supportive, and secure, and provides a loving environment for such sensitive and critical learning. In a classroom, they may feel that they have to look good in front of classmates and so they cannot be entirely honest about understanding or not understanding what they are learning. Also, some school programs spend less than one hour a year on this knowledge.

When appropriate, the "30 Simple Ways" in this book include role-playing suggestions. To play these educational games you ask your children a variety of questions about situations to see how they would react and what actions they would take. As you wait for their answer, don't be tempted to answer for them. It doesn't matter if children give the wrong answers, it's much safer if they make mistakes with you than in reality. Praise them when they are right. And when they are wrong, gently guide them to the correct answer. Because of the wonderful imaginations of children, "what if" games can even be fun. A story with my own eight-year-old son reflects this. One day while he helped me with the dishes, I asked him, "What if a man approached you and had a weapon?"

"I'd take a baseball bat and hit him," he said as he whipped the dish towel through the air.

"But there's no baseball bat around."

"Then I'd punch him in the gut," he said as he did a karate kick in the middle of the kitchen.

"But he's bigger than you. Why not just run away?"

"Because it's more fun to fight," he said, with a bold stance.

I explained that while it may look fun when kids beat up adults in the movies, in reality big people are much stronger than children. It would be best to run away.

A thoughtful expression crept over his face and he stopped jumping around. Looking up at me with a furrow across his brow, he said, "But an adult can run faster than me."

That's a natural question from a child. So I explained that when a child yells and starts running away, people will generally leave them alone. People who take children prefer children who go with them without a struggle. My son found this very reassuring. He gave me a big hug and went dashing out the door to get in some last minute basketball before nightfall. Whew! Another lesson slipped in, in the midst of a busy schedule. Just one of these lessons a night can be the foundation for your family safety program.

When playing "what-if" games, it's important not to stop too soon. If your child gives the right answers you may relax and think they understand. But this story from the

Sesame Street Parents' Guide shows that what your child understands may not be enough:

"A mother asked her child, 'If somebody came up to you and said that he'd lost his puppy, would you go and help him find the puppy?' The child said, 'No.' Then the mother asked, 'What if he lost his kitten? Would you help him find the kitten?' The child said, 'Yes,' and the mother asked, 'Why would you do that?' The child replied, 'Because kittens need more help than puppies do.'"

Another story, from SAFE-T-CHILD Director Trish Charron-Holt, also illustrates the value of not settling for the first answer your child gives. By pushing a little, you may reveal a clearer view of your child's actual perceptions of safety:

"A while ago I saw a program about the lures people use to abduct children. I got a transcript of the show and when it arrived my daughter was flipping through it. I decided to discuss it with her and we did a role-play using the 'photographer at the mall' lure. I asked her what she would do if someone approached her and said that she could be a model and offered to take her picture. Right away, she said she wouldn't go, that she would know better. But I kept pressing for her reactions to different approaches. I said, but what if the person told you he was giving out $100 bills to each person who agreed to be screen tested and you would get paid no matter what. The person also told you he had already paid four people today and all you had to do was come out to the van parked outside and smile. She thought for a few seconds and looked up at me with concern in her eyes. 'I would go,' she admitted. We both looked at each other and realized at that moment that we had a lot more work to do in the area of personal safety."

When role-playing with your children, follow these guidelines:

• As you ask questions, don't answer for your children; give them time to respond.

• If they make a mistake, gently guide them to the correct understanding and answers. Praise them when they give the correct response.

• Sometimes role-play in natural settings such as parks.

• When role-playing the various safety rules, make it a fun, special, and non-fearful experience for your child.

• Instruct your children to never play games with people they do not know.

• Play the games to their natural conclusions, giving your children time to look at the problem from many angles, so that you can discover the gaps in their logic.

• Once they know the safety rules, continue playing "what-if" games occasionally to reinforce and remind them about important safety rules. One father recommended video taping your children while role-playing so that they can see themselves in action later.

Teach By Example

Children model their parents' behavior. That's why you should demonstrate safety skills, especially when you are with your children. By being safety conscious yourself, you set a pattern for safety in your children's lives. To be truly effective, it is important that the personal safety rules are part of the overall rules that your family lives by. You can blend them into your day-to-day teaching just as you do the importance of brushing their teeth every night and turning off the burner on the stove.

Also, to make sure your children understand that the safety rules are to be taken seriously, you must honor them as well. For example, we teach children that they are in charge of setting the boundaries for physical attention with their body; so we must respect their wishes ourselves and stop hugging them when they pull away and stop tickling them when they say to stop. The following tips will help guide parents as they "teach by example" the important safety rules to their children:

1. **Children naturally need and enjoy affection, but let them set the limits.** With your child or other children, be aware of the child's level of comfort when you show them physical affection and respond accordingly.

2. **Do not force them to give or accept other people's physical attention.** Many adults love to hug and kiss children. However, a child may not actually enjoy it. You may have a hard time adjusting if they do not want to accept grandpa's kiss or Aunt Sue's hug, but you must give your child the right to decide what level of physical attention is comfortable for them.

3. **Always tell your children where you are going and when you will be back.** If you want your children to keep you posted on their comings and goings, parents should extend the same courtesy. It helps set a pattern for communication in your family.

4. **Do not ask children who are alone for directions or assistance.** Adults should not ask children for directions or assistance. Also, if a child you don't know starts to chat with you, ask the child's parent if it is okay to talk to their child and ask a child's parents before giving the child anything such as food or a toy.

5. **If you find a lost child act responsibly.** Keep the child with you in plain site and seek assistance from others to help find the child's parents. Reassure the child that people are helping them to find his or her parents.

The combination of music, role-playing, and teaching by example are the strongest tools parents can use to keep their children, and other children, safer.

The Bottom Line:
Your Child Must Do It

"Children who have been taught to think for themselves are the safest children of all."
   – The Safe Child Book, Sherryll Kerns Kraiser

"Don't wait for your child to be hurt. Make sure that they know everything they need to know and that they are going to be safe. Cause you're not going to be there when this happens. They're going to be alone."
   – "Child Hunters," CBS's *48 Hours*

"'Hundreds and hundreds of children are not abducted, because they are equipped with knowledge,' says Anne Cohn Donnelly, executive director of the National Committee to Prevent Child Abuse."
   – "Child Abductions: What a Mom Must Know," McCall's

The fact is that if it happens, it will almost always happen when you are not there. When faced with a dangerous or uncomfortable situation, your child will be on his or her own. The bottom line is: your child must have the knowledge, the skills, and the confidence to use his or her own judgment to keep him or herself safe.

It is hard to express how deeply encouraging it is to me that thousands of children each year get away from adults by using safety skills. Here are a few of their heartening stories:

- "Twelve-year-old Rebecca Savarese says she wasn't

afraid when a scruffy-looking man pointed a gun at her as she walked to school. But when he told her to get in a truck parked nearby, she thought, 'I have to get away' . . . When the man grabbed her backpack, Rebecca raced down the hill, screaming to a janitor, 'I almost got kidnapped!'"
– "Student Newsline," The Boston Globe

• "One day last fall, 11-year-old Amy Fraser and a friend went fishing at Willow Pond, a small park surrounded by big houses with broad lawns, a block from her home in suburban Willowbrook, Ill. A stranger drove up, watched the girls bait their hooks and cast their lines, then got out of his car and walked to the water's edge. That was all it took. 'We were scared and we just ran,' recalls Amy."
–"Never Talk to Strangers – And Watch Out for Nice Guys, Too," Newsweek

• "The girl was walking to a Girl Scouts meeting when she passed a Jeep parked at Sixth and Monroe streets. A man in a vehicle asked the girl to accompany him, but she turned and ran home. The man got out of the Jeep, followed the child to her house and knocked at the front door. He left when no one answered." – "Stranger in Black Jeep tries to Kidnap 7-year-old Girl," News Journal, Wilmington, DE

• ". . . a man driving a burgundy van like the one the molester sometimes uses called out to a seventh grader a block from (her school). She ran to some friends and reported the incident when she got to school." – "Stalking the Children," Newsweek

• "An old, beat-up pickup truck passed as she walked along, stopped and backed up, the father said his daughter told him. The driver said something like, 'Hey little girl, are you cold? Would you like a ride?' The girl started walking faster, and the truck followed. She ran to a nearby house. No one was home, so she hid behind a tree at the side of the house, she told her father. The truck disappeared." – "Attempted Abductions Make Twin Tiers Children Fearful," <u>Star-Gazette</u>

Children's best overall defense against abduction and sexual abuse is the following:

• a sense of their own rights

• a solid understanding of the safety rules outlined in this book

• the ability to accurately assess and handle a wide variety of situations

• knowing where and how to get help

• knowing they will be believed

Section One of this book was designed to help parents understand a difficult topic. And to help them realize why they must be involved in educating their children about the important – even lifesaving – safety rules. The next section presents the rules in an easy-to-read and easy-to-use format. These "30 Simple Ways" can be your child's door to safety.

30
SIMPLE
WAYS

TO HELP PREVENT
YOUR CHILD FROM
BECOMING LOST, MISSING,
ABDUCTED, OR ABUSED

You see I'd rather be safe
Than always polite
Your mom or dad will tell you
That night after night

"G.O.M.F." from *Can't Fool Me!*
Yello Dino Records

1

You Can Say
"NO!"

"In all Adam's small life we taught him not to take candy from strangers. All the things that we thought were appropriate. But we also taught him to respect authority figures unequivocally: that he should be a little gentleman. I think if we had put *more* emphasis on the fact that he had the right to say 'no,' maybe the outcome of his case might have been different . . . he might have been alive today if he wasn't such a little gentleman."

   — John Walsh, "How to Raise a Street Smart Kid," HBO

". . . he tricked his victims into going with him willingly. If a child just said **no** and made some noise, he left him or her alone."

   — "Child Abductions: What a Mom Must Know," McCall's

Children should understand that there are times when they do not have to be perfect little gentlemen and ladies. A child who can say "no" to an adult when he is uncomfortable or scared will be the child who has a chance to keep himself safe. Most parents like to think that they are raising polite children, but when a child's personal safety is being threatened a child should not have to worry about whether or not he is going to offend an adult or hurt an adult's feelings. What he should be able to focus on is: "Am I going to be safe if I do what this adult is telling me to do?"

Abductors often approach children with "lines," which are designed to short-circuit the child's instincts. These lines could include: "Can you help me find my puppy, Sammie?" or "You could be a model. Can I take your picture?" or "Can I help you tuck in your shirt?" If an adult approaches a child with a "line," the child's natural instincts or "gut" may be shouting "no." But the child's belief that adults must be obeyed can interfere with his ability to listen to his instincts. Because the child was raised to be respectful of adults, and to be kind and helpful, he may follow the adult's request. He may not even stop to think that he can refuse.

As parents, we have to make sure our children have our approval to say "no" when anyone attempts to do anything that does not feel right to the child. We should make sure children know that their personal safety is more important than being kind and obedient.

As part of understanding when it is okay to refuse an adult's request, your child should know that trustworthy adults normally do not ask children for assistance, such as asking for directions or carrying packages to a vehicle. Such seemingly harmless requests are being used by abductors to trap children.

**ACTION
STEPS**

1. Teach your child that it's better to be safe than polite.

By the age of two children have already discovered the power of the word "no." Direct this natural instinct in a positive way by teaching your children that they have the right to say "no" to adults who make them feel uncomfortable with their requests or touches. Teach your child that if someone gets too close, say "no." And if someone asks them to do something they don't usually do or that doesn't feel right, say "no." Then, they should get away and tell as quickly as possible.

2. Give them supporting statements.

Besides "no," teach children expressions that they can use when any person's actions make them uncomfortable. For example, they can say: "Please stop, I don't like that," or "That's not fun anymore; I don't want you to do that." To help get them comfortable with asserting themselves, you can role-play together. For example, you, a family member, or family friend can hug them tight or tickle them and they can use these types of phrases to stop you when they've had enough.

3. Test their ability to say "no."

To ensure that your children are comfortable saying "no," play "what-if" games. Ask them, for example,

39

what they would say if your neighbor came over and started tickling them and they didn't like it. Keep asking "what-if" questions like this until you are sure that your children feel comfortable expressing their feelings to adults. They should practice saying "no" in a clear, forceful voice. To help them further integrate the concept, you can even make a fun game of saying "no" in a variety of ways, such as saying "no" like a mouse or saying "no" like a lion.

4. Reassure them that you are on their side.

Assure your children that you will never be mad at them if they refuse a request for physical attention or appear to be rude to an adult in the process of keeping themselves safe. Let them know that you will handle the consequences if that adult is annoyed or mad, or if their feelings are hurt.

2

Identify Strangers

"Up until at least age 10, 'children may feel that someone is no longer a stranger even after a few seconds'."
 – "Missing Children: The Ultimate Nightmare," Parents

"If there was a lightning storm, would you go out and play? Of course not . . . People are like the weather . . . We have to look out for those human lightning storms that strike – and they use basic lines."
 – Kenneth Wooden (author of Child Lures Family Guide), *The Home Show*

Telling children to "stay away from strangers" is not an adequate safety rule in today's world.* For one thing, children's concept of strangers is often very different from ours. Here are a few ways that children might describe a stranger:

"A stranger looks mean."

"A stranger wears a black mask, like Darth Vader."

"A stranger is missing a lot of teeth and he sits around in a vacant lot all day."

"Creepy looking."

"Dirty."

"Bigger than most people."

These descriptions show that children's concepts of strangers are not accurate, which means that they are vulnerable to the persuasive dialogues of the truly dangerous people who look "nice" or "fatherly." Dangerous strangers

41

often look like fathers, uncles, aunts, teachers, and doctors – because that's exactly what they are. The fact is, the bad guys don't label themselves for us, and worse, they purposely work at being nice, helpful, and likable so that they can throw everyone off guard. This works, because typically children do not perceive an engaging adult as a stranger. Since most children are naturally friendly, they have to understand clearly these three guidelines:

1. A stranger is any person they do not know, including people they may see regularly, such as a store clerk or a neighbor.

2. A person's looks do not matter.

3. They must pay attention to an adult's behavior, and recognize when that behavior is wrong.

Parents should be encouraged by the fact that there are many cases of *attempted* abductions and *attempted* molestations where the children stayed safe and free from abuse because they stayed away from people they didn't know.

While we need to teach children an accurate concept of strangers, we do not have to scare them. One way to present this information in a non-fearful way is to explain to your children that <u>most</u> people are nice, but every so often there is a person who is not nice. Parents can explain this to children in a simple way, that children can understand, such as this: There are people who are hurting on the inside, but we can't see their hurt. Because a person is hurting, he hurts others. Since we cannot tell on the outside if a person is hurting or not, we need to stay away from any person we do not know.

---

* There is an overall misconception that "strangers" commit these crimes. However, the reality is that the majority of the danger does not come from a stranger but, in fact, comes from someone the child or family knows.

ACTION STEPS

1. Discuss who is and who is not a stranger.

Explain to your child that a stranger is any person he does not know. To help integrate this concept, run down a list of people with your child who he considers strangers: include people such as a neighbor down the street or one of your co-workers. One way to further help your child integrate this concept is to take a pile of pictures, including your family members and friends mixed up with clips of people from magazine pictures. One by one hold up a picture and ask your child if that person is a stranger. Discuss your child's responses and correct him when necessary. Be sure your child fully understands that anyone he does not know, no matter how attractive or friendly looking, is a stranger. Also, be sure your children understand that even if someone they don't know approaches them in a familiar surrounding, such as a school or church, it doesn't mean that the person is trustworthy. Abductors and abusers often hang out in places where children feel comfortable.

2. Gauge the concept of strangers to your child's age.

Since children under two cannot tell the difference between good and bad strangers, you must teach them not to run away from you in public. By age three, experts say that children can begin to distinguish between people with whom they can be

43

friendly and those with whom they can't. By five, parents can discuss with their children the difference between someone being friendly and someone making suspicious overtures. Through the age of six, instruct your children to ask for your approval before they talk to or go with a person they do not know. From seven to ten, they can respond with polite hellos to people they do not know, but should not engage in conversation. By eleven, they can engage in light conversation with adults they do not know, but should not allow the conversation to become too personal.

3. Explain that you cannot know a person from the outside.

Your child should understand that a person may look nice on the outside, but not be nice on the inside. To help explain this concept, discuss with your child how whether he has on his good school clothes or a scary Halloween costume, he is still the same good person on the inside. Just as with a costume, any person can change their appearance and hide what they are really like inside. Another way to explain this concept is to tell your child that even a perfect looking apple can have a worm inside.

4. Instruct your children to keep their distance from strangers.

Tell them not to talk to any person they don't know unless you or a guardian is with them; not to take anything from strangers, not even their own things (for example, if an adult they do not know picks up their jacket and tries to hand it to them); and not to go anywhere with people they do not know. Tell your child that if an adult asks for directions or help, he should tell them to ask another adult.

44

5. Let your children talk to strangers when you are together.

This will allow you to observe your child's behavior with people he doesn't know. You'll have the opportunity to see if he is overly open to people he doesn't know or if he is shy. This will also help you see which lures your child might be most vulnerable to.

6. Prepare your children to go to strangers for help.

While we want children to understand that they cannot be sure of the motives of people they do not know, we have to explain that there is a big difference between a person they do not know approaching them and they themselves going up to a person they do not know for assistance. If your child is ever lost, one of the best things he can do is go to a stranger for help. For example, if he is lost in an amusement park he can approach a security officer. But even in this situation, they have to be careful. That is why experts suggest lost children approach counter employees, a mother or grandmother with children, or a law enforcement officer for help. These are considered "safe" strangers to approach.

45

What if you see a guy in town
Who wants his puppy found
What do you do when he asks for help
And no one is around

Tricky people
                    Tricky, tricky people
Have pain down in their heart
Tricky people
You can't fool me
'Cause I'm too smart

"Tricky People" from *Can't Fool Me!*
Yello Dino Records

3

Beware Of Tricky People

"'The tactic used by abductors is to become a good person in the child's eyes . . . The abductor poses as a trustworthy person – someone working for a church, a policeman, a fireman, or a Santa-like figure giving a present'"
   – "A Terrified Generation?," Parents

"20/20's investigation of childhood abductions has shown that the lures used by criminals can be put into categories. Among them: assistance – request for directions, carrying packages, helping to find a lost dog – the variations are limitless, the criminals are cunning. Bribery – the age-old lure of candy has been joined by those involving drugs, alcohol, toys, motor-cycle rides. Authority – posing as truant officers, cler-gymen, even police officers. Emergency – 'your mommy is very sick, come with me to the hospital.' Again, the variations are endless."
   – "The Lures of Death," ABC NEWS' *20/20*

To keep your children safe from the adults who prey on children, you must teach them more than just, "Don't take candy from strangers." These days that simple lesson doesn't even begin to instruct children about all of the many "come-ons" adults use to engage them, to entice them, and to frighten them. As the child's guardian, you must first learn the lures these "tricky" people use, and then you should instruct your children how to never be "tricked." The reality of this topic may be overwhelming for many parents. But this section is designed to be supportive as well as instructive for you and your children.

The fact is, people who want to lure children have amazingly creative and effective ways to do it. Most often abductors and molesters do not use physical force. They don't have to. Lures work. Hundreds of abductors and molesters use them to attract children. These lures are cleverly designed to confuse children's natural instincts. Many children who have been hurt by strangers, were drawn into a trap that began with seemingly harmless requests.

Former police officer and child abuse investigator, Seth L. Goldstein, wrote the definitive book on child sexual abuse for child abuse investigators across the country. In his book, *The Sexual Exploitation of Children*, he describes the "methods of seduction" used by child abusers. He classifies them into 11 basic methods, which the abusers use. According to Goldstein, the abusers are typically not well organized; they simply use whatever lure "works." (This complete list is located in Appendix A.) Kenneth Wooden, a former *20/20* and *Sixty Minutes* reporter, who interviewed child molesters, abductors, and murderers in prison, arranges what he calls "lures" into 14 basic types. They are described in his *Child Lures Family Guide* as: affection, assistance, authority, bribery, ego/fame, emergency, fun and games, heroes, jobs, name recognition, playmates, pornography, threats and fear, and drugs.

The power of the tricks has been illustrated on television programs from *The Oprah Winfrey Show* to *ABC's 20/20*, where they have shown how easy it is to abduct a child – usually in under one minute. Experts say that abductors' "scripts" short-circuit children's natural innocence, kindness, and friendliness. For example, children like to be helpful. That's why John Wayne Gacy was able to lure 33 boys, whom he then molested and killed. He simply asked them for help and offered them money to carry

48

items to his vehicle; then he forced them inside.

The methods are so powerful that even children who have been educated by their parents or in safety classes to recognize these tricks have still been caught off guard. But take heart: parents can properly educate their children to recognize and steer clear of tricks. But first you have to know what they are. Examples of some common tricks include the following:

"I can make you famous."
"But no one ever warned her about 'photographers.' Someone should have because, according to Detective Stephen Irwin of the Metropolitan Toronto Police Force Sexual Assault Squad, a phony photographer act 'is something that is used with all age groups, even by serial offenders. Holding a camera is a way to get people's attention and get their guard down. It helps start a conversation and personalizes it. Often there's not even any film in the camera'."
– "Three Canadian Children," <u>Reward</u>, Paulette Cooper and Paul Noble

"Can you help me find my puppy?"
   "Why didn't you run away?"
   "Because he wanted me to find Shorty."
– Exchange between five-year-old and her mother, after the daughter went with a man claiming to have a lost puppy, "How to be Safe in America," ABC's *PrimeTime Live*

"Come with me, I know your parents."
"Seven-year-old Steven Stayner was abducted in Merced, California, by a man who lured him into a car by saying he was working for a church and was driving to Steven's house to ask his mother for a donation. After driving awhile, the abductor left the car pretending to phone Mrs. Stayner for permission to have Steven spend the night with him. Later, he told Steven that his parents didn't want him."
– "A Terrified Generation?," <u>Parents</u>

49

"I'm a police officer, and you have to come with me."
"I seen these two kids, getting in and out, in and out of parked cars. One of these kids had smashed out one of the headlights with his foot – just literally kicked it right out. I stopped and I got out of the car. And this car [his car] looked like a police car. I mean, it righteously looked like a police car. It had a Bearcat scanner, had a 40-channel digital readout CB. CB antennas, scanner antennas. I told them. I said, 'I'm going to take you to the police station.'"
"Did you have a badge?"
"Yeah, I had a badge all the way back to, you know, 18, I guess." – Exchange between convicted child abductor and a reporter, "The Lures of Death," ABC NEWS' *20/20*

"Let's go to my house and have some fun."
" 'All the kids on the block knew him . . . In fact, he bought bikes for them to ride. But they could never take them home.' Police said that was part of Allen's tactic to gain children's trust. He would befriend children by buying them clothes, toys, food and arcade tokens and tickets, police allege." – "Child Pornography Arrest Shocks Neighbors," Austin American Statesman

"Don't tell anyone or else. . ."
"'The reason my kids never told me was because he threatened to kill them and he showed them guns,' the mother said." – "Child Pornography Arrest Shocks Neighbors," Austin American-Statesman

For more examples of the methods used by abductors and molesters to lure children see the list in Appendix A, "The Tricks Used By 'Tricky People.'"

50

ACTION STEPS

1. Discuss with your children the kinds of "lures" used by tricky people.

Introduce your children by at least five years old about how they should not accept anything from a person they don't know, such as candy or money. Also, they should not go anywhere with a person they do not know, even to help find a lost puppy. By five or six years old, you can start introducing your children to the variety of approaches used by abductors and molesters, such as the ones listed here and in Appendix A. Do not feel that you need to go over every lure in one sitting. You can gradually work the lures into your children's safety lessons, for example, over a period of one month. Along with a description of the lures, tell your child that if any adult approaches them in any of these ways they should cut off the dialogue and get away from that person immediately.

2. Play "what-if" games thoroughly.

Ask your children what they would do if a person came up to them and asked for directions, asked for help to find a lost pet, or asked them if they wanted to play video games, etc. Be sure to play these "what-if" games thoroughly so that you know if your children truly understand the concept of lures. Remember the little girl mentioned in the "Education" chapter whose mother discovered that she would not help a man

51

find a lost puppy, but would help him find a lost kitten? If the mother had been satisfied with her daughter's first response, she would not have uncovered her daughter's weakness.

3. Warn your children about authority figures.

Because the use of authority to gain control of children is so pervasive (most child abductors in prison confess to owning fake law enforcement badges and official-looking uniforms or clothing), be sure to explain to your child how he should respond if a person representing himself as a law enforcement officer, security guard, park ranger, or other authority figure approaches him. Your child should politely tell the person that he has been instructed to call "911," his parents, or the local police station to verify the person's credentials. Legitimate officers will not be offended by this request.

4

Cut The Dialogue!

"Do not get into a conversation with them. As soon as they start to talk to you, get out of there . . . *Bam,* you're out of there . . . Get your knees in the breeze."
    – Detective J.J. Bittenbinder, "Street Smarts: Straight Talk for Kids, Teens & Parents," PBS

"You must be prepared to handle inappropriate behaviors immediately to let the abuser know that you will not tolerate abuse."
    – Denise Martin, founder of SAVVY!, Portland, Oregon

One of the most empowering messages regarding staying free from the lures of tricky people was presented by Detective J.J. Bittenbinder in his *Street Smarts* video and again on *The Jerry Springer Show.* He explains that, "Anytime you have a lure, and he [the abductor] starts the lure, it's a dialogue you have with the child. As soon as the dialogue starts the kid says 'no' and walks away. And I don't care what lure it is, it's over . . . You don't allow a dialogue." The more the dialogue continues, the more "engaged" the child becomes and the more easily he or she will be seduced by the "scripts" of the molester or abductor. But the child has one strong power, which will allow him to stop the lure in its tracks. If your child understands this one simple rule – cut the dialogue! – his chances of being "lured" by strangers is reduced dramatically.

If a stranger comes to you
And starts to lay a rap
Don't hang around
Don't fall for his trap

"G.O.M.F." from *Can't Fool Me!*
Yello Dino Records

The message of "cutting the dialogue" brings with it a source of power for the child. Children are at an extreme disadvantage compared to an adult's size and mental capability. A child may think "How can I stay safe? What power do I have over a big adult?" They may be smaller than an adult, but they still have power. They have eyes to see, ears to hear, a voice to yell, legs to run, and feelings to trust. Children should understand that they have those powers and that being smart is better than being big and tough.

You've got your eyes that can see
You've got your ears that can hear
You've got your heart that can feel
You've got your feet that can get up
And run like the wind

"G.O.M.F." from *Can't Fool Me!*
Yello Dino Records

When children understand that they have the choice to "cut the dialogue" and use their powers to stay away from "tricky people," they will understand that they <u>can</u> keep themselves safe.

ACTION STEPS

1. Instruct your child how and when to "cut the dialogue."

The rules regarding talking to strangers apply here: if a person they do not know tries to start a conversation with them your child should "not make the connection." Instead, they should do whatever they have to do to "cut the dialogue." They should look away, walk away, and, if necessary, yell for help and run away.

2. Test your child's ability to "cut the dialogue."

Practice a variety of engaging "lines" that might attract your child to respond, such as "That's a cool skate board you're using, where did you get it?" or "You're so pretty. Have you ever modeled?" Then, have your child show you how they would "cut the dialogue" and get out of there.

5

My Body's Mine!

"One father said, 'I love kissing my darling three-year-old daughter good night, but sometimes she just looks up at me with a naughty little face and says, 'No kisses.' It can be really hard to respect her wishes when I love her so much, especially if I'm about to go out of town. But I know this is the best thing to do.'"
  – "Boundaries With People We Know," <u>KIDPOWER Guide</u>, Irene van der Zande

My body's mine
          Mine, mine
My body's mine
          Mine, mine
I'm no fool
I play by the rules
'Cause I know my body's mine

"My Body's Mine" from *Can't Fool Me!*
Yello Dino Records

Children should understand that their body is theirs, and that means that they can choose the level of physical affection that feels comfortable to them. Once they understand this rule, they will be better able to resist if they are ever approached by people intending to harm them. Too often, abduction or molestation starts with an adult who touches a child in a seemingly innocent way, such as by playing games that involve touching.

Children have a natural sense of appropriate and inappropriate touching. For example, they readily accept hugs and kisses from family members, but do not from people they do not know. Sometimes parents may worry that by addressing the issue of physical abuse they will take away their children's natural friendliness or affection. But there is a great difference between affection and abuse. When touching crosses over from one to the other, children sense the difference. It's our responsibility to give them information and direction so that they can keep themselves free from inappropriate touching.

Too often, parents unwittingly create mixed messages in children when they force them to kiss grandpa or put up with tickling from a neighbor. Children have to know that touching for the sake of teasing, play, or affection is always a choice. They must be able to set the limits on physical affection and touching such as being kissed, hugged, or tickled.

> *Just the other day*
> *A lady came up to me*
> *She said, "This is the cutest little guy*
> *That I have ever seen"*
> *And then she hugged*
> *So tight my air was gone*
> *So I said, "No! That hurts me so"*
> *And sang my body song*
>
> "My Body's Mine" from *Can't Fool Me!*
> Yello Dino Records

The important thing is to have clear agreements that a child has a right to stop unwanted touching or teasing. If children can set boundaries about minor intrusions, such as being hugged too tightly or being tickled, they can use that same skill to set boundaries before sexual abuse ever occurs. Even as parents, if we're not sure if our touch is wanted by the child, we should ask their permission.

ACTION STEPS

1. Tell your children that their bodies are theirs.

Discuss with your children that they have rights with regards to their body. They have the right to say who touches them and how; this includes Grandma Jane's cheek pinches, Uncle Fred's hugs, and even your kisses. It can be frightening and confusing for children to try and deal with setting boundaries with people they have learned to love. One way to help them understand appropriate boundaries is to tell children explicitly that it is not okay for someone to play with their private parts; in fact, it is against the law.

2. Teach children the difference between good touch and bad touch.

Parents should tell children that the parts of their body covered by their underwear and bathing suits are special. Tell them that it is not okay for someone older than them to touch them or ask to touch their private parts. They can touch themselves there but, generally, other people should not. With your child, discuss the natural situations where an adult may have to touch his or her private parts. Let your child help you name some examples of touches that are okay, such as when a parent has to help a child clean himself or check him for any medical reason, and of course to help answer any questions the child may have. A baby-sitter or relative may have to help a child clean himself or take them to the bathroom. Also, a doctor or nurse may need to touch the child's private parts for medical reasons.

3. Help your children overcome their natural embarrassment.

Often children won't say anything when they don't like physical attention because they are too embarrassed, especially if it involves people they know. As a parent you have to help them understand that their safety and comfort is more important than anyone else's embarrassment. Also, discuss that they should not feel bad if someone else acts like the child is hurting their feelings by not allowing forced physical affection. Reassure your child that you will deal with the consequences if the adult gets mad.

4. Tell children that it's okay to change their minds.

If they liked grandma's hugs yesterday, but do not today, that is okay.

5. Teach children how to stop uncomfortable touching.

When they don't like the way they are being touched, your children should be able to say, "No," along with phrases such as, "Would you please stop touching me like that?," "I don't like that," or "Leave me alone." The child can be instructed to add emphasis to their words with body language such as moving away from the person.

6. Instruct them to "tell" when an adult will not stop touching them.

They should know that people who don't respect their wishes not to touch their body are breaking the safety rules. If your child gets in a particularly difficult situation he can say, "Stop or I'll tell." Then your child should definitely tell you or someone he trusts. If he has no other option, your child could call "911" or "0" to get help right away. To help your child get used to telling people to stop touching him, you could have family members or friends pat your child's head, pinch his cheek, or pull him on to their laps. Let your child get comfortable with stopping the physical contact.

6
Trust Your Instincts

"The most important thing we come across when we talk about staying strong and free – if it feels bad on the inside . . . then something's not right and we need to get help."
  – "Kids and Strangers," WKRC-TV 12, Cincinnati

Well wouldn't you know
I saw this stranger in the mall
He looked real nice
But I thought twice
And you know that I said 'NO!'
And then I moved
At least three steps back
In my heart was a bell
So I ran to tell
And I sang my song like that

"My Body's Mine" from *Can't Fool Me!*
Yello Dino Records

Among the reported cases of attempted child abductions are thousands of children who listened to their "instincts" and steered clear of danger. "Instinct" is that deep, nagging, and uncomfortable feeling that we get in our stomachs telling us that danger might lie ahead. Instinct conjures up our natural "fight or flight" response, and can enable children to avoid danger and avert personal harm. For example, a child may get a "funny" feeling if a man in a car seems to be following him or if a coach seems to be touching him a little too often.

Children can sense danger. In fact, with sexual abuse children often "sense" that something is wrong before abuse actually occurs. When children learn to trust their "instincts" and to speak up, they are able to stop abuse before it even begins. As parents, you must give children the ability and skills to make abuse stop and to get help. You should encourage your children to trust their natural alarm systems. In fact, a child's natural instinct deserves respect – it is one of the most important tools for prevention of abduction and sexual abuse.

Children will appreciate knowing that when they get that funny feeling inside it is a power – like a friend – that can help them stay safe. So even if they are smaller than the person who is bothering them, they still possess a strong power to stop the situation.

> *So when your light says something's wrong*
> *You should act - not wait too long*
> *When you're feeling all alone*
> *You have the power to be strong*
>
> *You touch the light down in your heart*
> *It's so easy – just a thought*
> *It's the same around the world*
> *For every guy and every girl*
>
> "We Trust Our Feelings" from *Can't Fool Me!*
> Yello Dino Records

Another inner alarm system that can help children stay safe is their "little voice" or conscience. While the "gut" is screaming, "Let's get out of here!," the "little voice" is insisting, "This is not right." The gut signals danger and the little voice tells us that something is right or wrong. Your child can learn to trust this inner voice. By respecting the combination of "instinct" and the "little voice," children will be using their natural powers to keep themselves safe.

62

ACTION STEPS

1. Teach children to trust their instincts and their "little voice."

They usually experience instinct in their stomach or "gut" and their little voice in their head or heart. Explain that these are not imaginary feelings, but real feelings that they might get when something scares them or doesn't feel right. If someone makes them feel uncomfortable or funny inside, they should be told not to ignore that feeling but to act on it. Tell your children that even if they aren't 100 percent sure that trouble is about to occur, if they feel scared or unsure it's always smart to make a move. For example, if a car is getting too close or they feel they are being followed they should act immediately. For example, they could turn and run in the opposite direction.

2. Tell them you will back them up if their inner alarm system (instinct) ever goes off.

They should immediately do whatever they have to do to keep themselves safe. Reaffirm that you will respect their feelings. After all, if you don't trust their feelings, how can you expect them to?

7

Take Three Steps Back

"The first thing we have to do to maximize the safety of our children when they are not in the presence of a caretaking adult is to teach them to stay an *arm's reach plus* away from people they don't know even if they have to back up to do it."

– "Preventing Abuse and Abduction by Strangers," <u>The Safe Child Book</u>, Sherryll Kerns Kraiser

Take three steps back
Take three steps back
That's how you can begin
Take three steps back
Take three steps back
Then run like the wind

"Tricky People" from *Can't Fool Me!*
Yello Dino Records

Many abductors have caught their victims simply by reaching out and grabbing them. Teach your children to stay at least three arm lengths away from any adult they do not know. The reason children need to stay at this distance is because they cannot tell by appearances if a person is nice or not – and they need to keep themselves safe. This is a simple safety rule, but very effective.

Also, research shows that cars are involved in 80 percent of the cases where children are taken. Many abductions have occurred when adults call children over to their cars and, for example, ask for directions. When the child gets close enough the adult grabs their arm and pulls them in the vehicle. Crime experts say that the average adult simply does not ask children for directions. Therefore, if a child is approached for directions, this is a big "red flag." Your child should keep their distance!

ACTION STEPS

1. Teach children to stay at least three steps away from anyone they do not know.

If someone they don't know approaches them, they should back up. This safety rule is easier for children to visualize if you demonstrate it. Practice with role-playing games. You can be the stranger. Have your children demonstrate moving three steps back until they get it right.

2. Instruct your children to keep their distance if an adult asks them for help or directions.

They can either ignore the adult, say they don't know, tell the adult to go ask another adult for help, or just run away.

8

Yell! Yell! Yell!

"The only thing that might have saved Polly that night, says her aunt Juliete, is if she and her friends had screamed for help . . . 'Children need to learn to resist and scream no matter what.'"
   – "America's Child," <u>People</u>

"Do your children a favor. Encourage them to scream. It is an important defense tool. Don't raise a silent victim. You owe this to your children."
   – Letter writer to *Dear Abby*

Children have a natural talent for yelling – and they can use this talent to protect themselves. Too often, from the time children are little, adults tell them not to yell. But when in trouble a child who yells may be the safest child. Screams are meant to alert others to danger, whether real or imagined.

Parents should encourage their children to scream if they are ever in danger, and parents should prepare children to use this self-defense technique whenever they need it. Child abductors in prisons today say that if their potential victims made any noise, they left them alone. Surely we do not know if screaming would have saved some of the abducted children such as Polly Klaas, but perhaps it would have provided an opportunity for someone to attempt to save them. Experts advise parents to tell their children: yell as loud as you can; yell as hard as you can; yell to attract someone to help you; yell to scare the perpetrator away.

66

Another barrier to the effectiveness of this powerful safety tool is a child's embarrassment. Children don't like the idea of making fools of themselves or of drawing attention to themselves, especially as they get older. But if they are being abducted, attention from a helpful adult is exactly what they need. They must understand that it is better to be safe than worried about being embarrassed.

As well as screaming, children must also learn to yell out key phrases, such as "This is not my father!" This is critical because if a child is being taken from a public area, passersby may just think the child is throwing a temper tantrum. The dramatic case in England where two adolescent boys abducted a toddler from a mall is a heart-wrenching example. People in the mall that day said that they did, in fact, remember the two boys leading a crying child outside, but they assumed he was just the brother of one of the boys. Shortly after that, the child was murdered. If the child had yelled, "This is not my brother!" he may have been saved.

ACTION STEPS

1. Train your children to make a verbal commotion if anyone ever tries to grab them.

Your children should practice yelling so that they can break into a guttural yell at any moment. They should also practice yelling specific descriptive statements such as: "I need help!," "This is not my father!," and

"I'm being kidnapped." Without practice a child may be too scared at the moment to conjure up the energy to really yell. They must learn how to yell. It seems simple, but almost no one does it right at the moment they really need it.

2. Explain to them that safety is more important than embarrassment.

If your children resist yelling because they feel silly or are embarrassed, explain to them that it is much more important to save themselves if anyone ever bothers them than it is to worry about being embarrassed for a few minutes. Tell children that their voice is one of their powers over bigger people who may be bothering them. Explain to them that many children have foiled abductors by scaring them away with a long, loud scream from the gut.

9
Run Like
The Wind

"The point is that nowadays, even in Willowbrook, to run like hell from a suspicious stranger is the right thing for a kid to do."
  – "Never Talk to Strangers – And Watch Out for Nice Guys, Too," <u>Newsweek</u>

Take three steps back
Take three steps back
That's how you can begin
Take three steps back
Take three steps back
Then run like the wind

"Tricky People" from Can't Fool Me!
Yello Dino Records

While frequently the news is filled with stories of missing children, often overlooked are the stories of the attempted abductions, of the children who got away. When these stories are reported by media, we usually find that the reason the children got away was because they followed basic safety skills. Running is one of these basic skills. The success stories often include children who trusted their instincts when they felt scared, and who *ran* to a safe place.

In one example, from a 1994 *Newsweek* article, two girls were playing by a pond near their homes in Illinois. When a stranger driving by slowed down and began watching them, the girls ran. One of the girls said, "I was upset we had to leave but I knew it was the right thing to do."

In addition to running, children should also understand that: if they feel scared and decide to run to safety they can do anything necessary to get away, even dropping their school books or a back pack, so that they will not be slowed down. In his *Street Smarts* video, Detective J.J. Bittenbinder advises parents to tell their children that if they are ever threatened they should "drop the books and run." He tells the story of one little girl whose father had told her to never lose her school books or she would be punished. So one day, while a man cornered and molested her, she hung onto her new school books. Children should know that their safety is more important than any book, clothing, or other personal item. Things can be replaced; your child cannot.

ACTION STEPS

1. Tell your children to run to a safe place if they are scared.

Advise them to run to the nearest public place such as a fast food restaurant or to a place where there are other people. They should also know the "safe houses" along any route that they travel regularly. If someone is following them in a vehicle, generally they should turn and run in the opposite direction that the vehicle is going or to the nearest safe place, depending on the circumstances. To help scare the person away and get other people's attention, they should also remember to yell while running.

70

2. Make sure that your children are not embarrassed to run.

You can test their willingness to actually run (while yelling) at a park or in your neighborhood.

3. Check their safety knowledge with "what-if" games.

Periodically, as your children grow up, quiz them to see what they would do in specific situations. Make sure at some point that their answer is that they would run if they were scared.

4. Don't reinforce the wrong messages.

Don't, for example, tell your children to never lose or damage their belongings such as school books. Their safety should always come first. Help your children be a tough target by telling them not to hesitate if they feel scared. They should drop their school books, backpack, or whatever they are carrying – and run. They should also know that if they drop their personal items, they will provide a trail of evidence that you can use to find them.

10
Break Away!

"'I don't care if they have a weapon – *don't* go with them. Kick, scream, break things, scratch, go for the crotch, the eyeballs . . . *anything*.'"
> – Scared mother's advice to her 10-year-old daughter, "Fears of the Unspeakable Invade a Tidy Pink Bedroom," <u>Newsweek</u>

"I wasn't scared of the gun, I was just scared to get into that pick-up truck."
"Had you thought what might happen if you did get into that pick-up truck?"
"I wouldn't be here talking to you."
> – Exchange between 12-year-old who broke away from an abductor, NBC's *Today Show*

Many parents are signing up their children for martial arts courses, because they believe that with those skills their children will be able to better defend themselves against attackers. In fact, experts including law enforcement officers and martial arts masters, say that almost without exception children will not be able to physically defend themselves against an attack by an adult. Actually, the primary benefit of developing martial arts for children is the confidence and self-esteem they gain from the mental and physical discipline.

While children cannot "beat up" an adult, that is not to say that they should not put up a struggle if they are ever grabbed. In fact, many children have gotten away from attackers by biting, kicking, and spitting, while yelling their heads off the whole time. Most convicted child abductors have said that they leave children alone the minute they make any noise or fight back. Therefore, your children should know that that in some situations they should put up a fight and try to break away. Sometimes a child's odds are much better if he resists than if he does not. However, some perpetrators get more violent if they are angered. So the best safety education provides your child with the reassurance that they can make the right decision in a specific situation. They should be able to judge when to fight, when to make a scene, and when to be quiet and wait for an opportunity to run. If they have knowledge they will be better prepared to do this.

In most situations, rather than worrying about physically defending themselves, children should, as one police officer stated, use their heads – and *stay away* from any threatening situation. Sensei David Ham says that an objective in Aikido, a non-violent martial art, is to understand "ma-ai" or distance. A child should keep their distance no matter what. If they are ever approached, they should first "take three steps back," then, if it feels wrong, "yell, yell, yell" for help, and "run like the wind" to safety. In one case, a 12-year-old escaped from a potential abductor because she followed the advise her mother gave her every morning before she left for school: "God forbid someone grabs you, but if they do – kick, punch, bite, spit. Do what you have to to get away." In this case, the potential abductor grabbed the girl's backpack. She faked a seizure, and while pretending she had to sit down, she wiggled out of her backpack and ran.

ACTION STEPS

1. Tell your children to break away if anyone grabs them.

They should not wait to struggle and put up a fight; they should do it right away to scare off the attacker. The first stage of an attempted abduction is the point where the attacker is the most vulnerable, unsure of himself, and subject to surprise. Adult self-defense classes instruct women to repel an attacker by engaging in activities that will throw the person off-guard such as pretending to vomit or faking a seizure.

2. Practice letting your children "break away" from you.

Grab one of your children and have them struggle and fight to get free. This will show them that strength alone is not enough.

3. Remind your children to practice safety skills so that they will never be grabbed in the first place.

All of the safety rules presented in this book will help children use their heads and steer clear of dangerous situations.

4. Instruct your children to not allow themselves to be put in a vehicle or to be taken anywhere.

They should do whatever they must do to avoid this. If a person tells them to be quiet, to come with them and they won't be hurt, that person is lying. Experts say that abductors like to take children away from public places to a place that is private and to a place where they will be in control.

5. Instruct your children to never go with a person holding a weapon.

While this is a really tough point to address, keep in mind that if a child is threatened by an attacker with a weapon and the child goes, his chances of survival are much lower than if he had put up resistance from the very start and got away.

*You don't touch me there
'Cause I will run and tell
It's against the law
And I'll tell what I saw
And sing my body song*

"My Body's Mine" from *Can't Fool Me!*
Yello Dino Records

11

Tell Until
Someone Listens

"Part of the process was I would pick children that were non-assertive, that I knew wouldn't tell."
   – Convicted child molester, NBC's *The Crusaders*

"Now, consider: If children valued their sexuality as much as (or more than) their bicycles, and if they realized that sexual abuse is like having their bicycle stolen, then abuse would be reported (and resisted whenever possible) without hesitation."
   – Abuses to Sexual Abuse Prevention Programs, Jan Hindman, The Hindman Foundation

In one reported abuse case which aired on ABC NEWS' *20/20*, a young girl was molested by a trusted family member for two years. She finally overcame her fears and told someone, and the person was tried and jailed. By telling, she got the abuse to stop. Now her advice to other kids is: "If no one listens to them, they should keep on telling until someone will listen to them." This should be every parent's advice to their own children.

Children may be reluctant to tell their parents about unusual situations with adults, such as being followed or touched inappropriately. Part of the problem is that children often feel that when they reveal something bad they will be yelled at or punished, just as they would be if they broke or damaged something in their home. But they should understand that if this situation should ever occur it is not their fault and they will not be punished.

Parents should carefully respond to children's fears. For example, if your child tells you that someone was following him home from school, you should not focus on correcting him for not following the correct path home. Instead, provide a nurturing context for him to discuss high-risk situations. Each time we listen to our children and believe them, we teach them that their feelings and telling the truth are more important than making mistakes. Although they may need correction too, the fact that they had the courage to tell the truth is really more important. At the very least, let your children know that you will reduce your disciplinary actions for any mistakes they made, such as taking the wrong path home. This can help give them the confidence to discuss very serious situations, should they arise in the future.

Reports say that girls report molesters four to one over boys. Why? Two reasons. One, boys are more susceptible to embarrassment. Boys do not like to admit to themselves, their friends, or their families that anything like this could have happened to them. The stigma of the action is too great for them to bear. And two, because boys fear that if their parents become worried about them they will respond by placing more restrictions on them, according to Kenneth Wooden on ABC's *The Home Show*. Boys resist being more closely supervised, so they don't tell their parents about things that bother them. But this kind of thinking could mean trouble. One young boy had been bothered repeatedly by a man during his morning paper route. He told his younger brother that a guy was "bugging" him, but made his brother promise not to tell his parents. Two weeks later he was abducted and murdered.

To get children not to tell, abusers often threaten children. They will use a variety of threats such as, "Your parents won't believe you," "I'll kill your puppy," or "Your mother won't hug and kiss you anymore." Children need to know that most threats are hollow, that you will always love them, and that they have to tell no matter what. Even if they get the person to stop bothering them, the abuser will usually go looking for another child. If your child tells, then there is a chance that the abuser will be caught and stopped. Also, it is important to tell authorities so that the potential abuser can be found.

Unfortunately, all children may not be able to resist the sexual advances of a determined adult. If we teach them to first say, "no," and then tell, they at least have a chance to be successful in half of the task. When a child who has been abused tells right away, he is more likely to have a quick and successful recovery.

ACTION STEPS

1. Give your children the power to tell.

As soon as your children are vocal, make them understand that they have to tell a trusted adult if anyone is touching them or scaring them. They should tell if someone asks them to keep a secret, gives them money or a gift, makes them feel uncomfortable, or threatens them. Instruct your children to tell especially if an adult tells them not to tell and if the adult threatens them in any way. If your children are not sure if an adult's behavior is "bad," let them know that they can ask you and you will help them decide. Also, make sure they understand that it is better to tell you or someone else later than not to tell at all.

2. Encourage your children to be firm with a potential abuser.

Children should be taught to say "no" to a person who is bothering them. Then if the adult doesn't stop they should say, "Stop or I'll tell on you."

3. Instruct your children to look for help until they get it.

To be sure your children know who they can go to for help. Describe a variety of scenarios and ask them who they would talk to in each case. For example, ask your children who they would tell if a man followed them to school and tried to talk to them. They should decide if they want to tell their mother, father, aunt, minister, teacher, or some other adult. Ask them who they would talk to if the first person they go to isn't available. Children should also know that it is never too late to tell and ask for help, even months or years later.

4. Teach your children to tell if they see anything suspicious.

Children should be watchful and aware of potentially dangerous situations, for example, someone hanging around the school playground. They should try to describe the person as best as they can including height, size, color of hair, the type of car they are driving, and the license plate number. They can even write the license plate number in the dirt. Children have often been the ones to successfully describe suspicious people. You can practice testing your child's memory by periodically asking them to glance at some adult, then turn around and describe them. You can even make a game of memorizing license plates, car colors, and descriptions.

12

Don't Keep
Bad Secrets

"Since 85 to 90 percent of perpetrators are known to the children, sexual abuse cannot take place without secrecy. Therefore, one of the first things a potential perpetrator will do is find out if the child can keep a secret. If a child steadfastly refuses, most abusers will not risk moving ahead."
> – "Preventing Sexual Abuse," <u>The Safe Child Book</u>, Sherryll Kerns Kraiser

Sexual abuse cannot take place without secrecy. Teaching your children the importance of not keeping secrets will protect them from the majority of abuse situations that they might encounter. In fact, children should be taught that there should be no secrets in your family. Touching, especially, should never be a secret.

Secrecy is the main reason why abuse occurs over a long period of time with so many children. Secrecy strengthens the adult's power and control over the child, isolates the child from others, and helps continue the physical abuse. Potential abusers may use lines such as, "We won't tell anyone about our private game, okay?" If an adult requests that the child keep a secret, that is the "alert" for trouble. Children should know that anyone who tries to get them to keep quiet about something they are doing is not a friend, even if mom or dad has referred to them as a friend in the past. Children should also be warned that abusers will use threats such as saying, "Go ahead and tell, no one will believe you." Abusers have been known to threaten to hurt a child, his pet, or his loved ones unless he keeps a secret. But children should know that those threats are usually hollow.

Abusers also may twist the concept of secrecy to make the child feel that they are a "partner" in the sexual activity. According to author Jan Hindman, in *Abuses to Sexual Abuse Prevention Programs*, molesters might use lines such as:

"Do you have any idea what your mother would do if she knew the kinds of touching <u>we've</u> been doing?"

"If your breasts hadn't grown, I would never have allowed you to touch me like this."

"I could tell that you like this or I never would have done it."

"Because I love you so much, I won't tell your mother what you've been doing with me."

These approaches, which are almost too difficult for a normal, loving parent to hear, make it painfully clear why you must be sure your child will not keep bad secrets.

Sometimes children may not confide in adults about troubling situations because they do not want to "tattle" or because they are afraid their parents will be angry with them or will not believe them. Children should feel confident that you will believe them. Parents should understand that children will not always tell about abusive situations in a direct manner. For example, if Uncle Bill is touching their private area, your child may say to you, "Uncle Bill is ugly." Parents should try to really listen to their children and understand what they may really mean when they make comments about, act uncomfortable, cry, or hide around a particular adult.

ACTION STEPS

1. Teach your children from a young age that there are no secrets in your family.

They should not keep secrets from you, especially secrets about an adult who is bothering them or trying to get them to keep a secret. Encourage your child to share any secret that an adult asks them to keep. Instruct your children that if an adult tries to get them to keep a secret or says something like, "You don't need to tell your mom and dad, I'll tell them later," your child's response should be: "No, I don't keep secrets and I'm going to tell."

2. Explain that whispering and secrets with friends are okay, as long as they are not dangerous.

Children may confuse secrets with whispering, with surprises (like birthday gifts), or with secrets between friends such as friendship clubs. Children should be taught the difference between okay secrets, which are fun and harmless, and bad secrets, which could hurt them or someone else if they don't tell. Surprises are things that make people happy and that get told eventually, whereas secrets are never told.

3. Teach children that there is a difference between privacy and secrecy.

Privacy means keeping something to yourself, and deserves respect. This might include your feelings about a friend or a poem you wrote, but don't want anyone to read. Secrecy means that you are bound not to tell. If there is pain, shame, or embarrassment surrounding the secret, something is wrong.

4. Help children understand that a bad touch is not their fault.

If someone touches them in a way that is not okay and makes them feel uncomfortable, tell your children that you will always love them and that you will not be mad at them for what happened. Also, reassure them that you will deal with the adult who harmed them and that they don't have to.

13

Always
Ask First

"Don't go anywhere with anyone unless your mother or father or another adult they have told you to trust says it's OK every time."

— "Strangers," <u>The KIDPOWER Guide</u>, Irene van der Zande

How can parents make sure children are safe when they can't be with them all of the time? One way is to teach your children to communicate with you. Children should understand that to be safe their parents or guardians need to know where they are at all times, so children should always ask their parents or guardians first before going anywhere.

Children should also know that they can call their parents if they ever need a way to get home from wherever they are. To reinforce this rule and honor their children, parents should also call their children and communicate with them when they are away from home.

ACTION STEPS

1. Teach your children to always ask your permission.

Before going anywhere, whether it's to a friend's

house, to help a neighbor, or to the store, children should ask an adult. They should also tell you or their caregiver if their plans change for any reason. To make sure they understand this safety rule, ask them to identify all of the various situations where it is important for them to check first with you before they go anywhere or do anything.

2. Give your children a checklist of approved adults.

Children need clear guidelines about which adults they are allowed to go somewhere with without checking first, such as their school teachers or grand-parents. Have your children practice saying, "I'll check with my mom first," whenever anyone who is not on your "approved" list asks them to go somewhere. You should always be on time to pick up your child from anywhere, such as school, sports, or dance classes. The child who lingers alone is more vulnerable to abductors.

3. Be sure that you keep in touch with your children when you are apart.

To make this safety rule a family rule, you should let your children know where they can reach you by phone. When you are traveling, you should leave an itinerary with your children.

4. Teach your children to call if they ever need a ride home.

For example, if a friend's parent was supposed to take your child home and suddenly could not make the trip, your child should call you. Tell him that you will find a way to get him home and that he should not try to make his own arrangements.

14
Use The Telephone

"'Children who don't know their address and phone number are missing a major defense if they should get lost . . . They have no way of getting home or calling for help.'"
– "Careful, Not Fearful," <u>Sesame Street Parents' Guide</u>

It really is so simple
It's actually fun
"O" for Operator
Or dial 9-1-1
Say your name and problem
Say your address too
Sing your phone number
I'm so proud of you

"Help Me Operator" from *Can't Fool Me!*
Yello Dino Records

Once a six-year-old girl was abducted by a man who asked her for directions then pulled her into his car. After 48 hours of frantic searching by the community, including posters and newscasts of the incident, the man got scared and dropped the child off in town – right next to a telephone. The girl knew to call "911" for emergencies and the police picked her up right away.

Like this little child, all children need to know how to use the telephone and they need to memorize important telephone numbers. They also need to know their full name, their parents' names, and their address. And they need to know how to call "911" or "0" for the operator to get help. They should be instructed how to use all types of telephones, including pay phones, office phones, and hotel phones. And they should know to never call "911" to make a prank call. Remember, music is one of the easiest ways to teach children to memorize information such as their telephone number. Many parents have said that they just couldn't get their children to remember their area code and home phone number until their numbers were set to music.

Many parents teach their children their home telephone number, but forget that they also need the area code. If a child is abducted, he or she can easily be transported into another area code or out-of-state. While searching for their missing children, parents have been known to call their telephone number at every area code to see if their missing child has called.

ACTION STEPS

1. Teach your children your telephone number including your area code as soon as they become verbal.

Music is such an effective tool for this purpose. You can make up your own little song or purchase sing-along music such as Yello Dino's *Can't Fool Me!* album. The song, "Help Me Operator," is especially designed to make it easy for children to remember their telephone numbers (as well as learn to dial "9 1 1" or "0"). Older children should also memorize their parents' work number and the number of a trusted neighbor or family member. Also, keep these numbers written down near your home phone. Additionally, children should know their address and their parents' or guardians' full name.

2. Teach children that they can dial "9-1-1" or "0" for emergencies (or other emergency numbers in some areas).

Some experts believe it is better to call "9 1 1" or "0" even before calling home. Calling home might actually slow things down in many cases. Dialing an emergency number is almost sure to get fast help. If "9 1 1" in your area has advanced services, the operators will have the address and phone number or the call will appear on their screens. Be sure that young children do not confuse "9 1 1" with "nine-eleven." Since there is no number "1 1" on the dial they may get confused. Additionally, children should know that they can dial the operator (in most places) without money and reverse the charges. When your child calls for an emergency, instruct him to give his name, problem, and address to the operator who answers. The information and how it is delivered by the child helps the operator evaluate whether the call is genuine or a prank. Children should be warned to never call to play "emergency pranks." When they really need help, they might not be believed.

3. Teach your children how to dial from several kinds of phones.

Home phones, pay phones, hotel phones, and business phones all work differently. You don't want your child's efforts to reach you thwarted because they didn't know how to use the only telephone that was available. For example, hotel phones often require the caller to dial "9" or "8" first, and business phones require that you first select an outgoing line. In hotels, you can dial "0" to get the hotel operator who will then dial "911." You must actually practice with your child on real phones, not just verbally explain how to use them.

4. Plan ahead for emergencies.

If your child feels threatened in his home, one trick is to dial "911" and leave the phone off the hook. The operator will be able to hear everything, learn the source of the call, and dispatch help.

15
Always Have
A Buddy

"Children who are alone make easy targets for strangers."
– "Careful, Not Fearful," <u>Sesame Street Parents' Guide</u>

We've all heard that children should use the buddy system. But it is such a simple idea that we tend to overlook it. It can be a valuable preventative tool for a child for several reasons: 1. an abductor is often looking for a child who is alone, 2. if there is a problem the second child can go for help, 3. when two or more children are together they are more likely to make the right decision, and 4. two children are much more difficult for an abductor to deal with than one. The buddy system should be a family rule. Chil-

dren should always be with another person when they are away from home.

Using the buddy system means staying together. Police and martial arts instructors teach that when a person is just 21 feet away from another person it may be too much distance to help.

ACTION STEPS

1. Make it a family safety rule for children to have a buddy.

Whenever they go anywhere, such as to a playground, to the mall, or to a public restroom, your child should be with someone. Make sure your child understands that it is safer to be with others when they go places. If anything happens, a friend will be there to help. One special note: children should *always* use a buddy (preferably an adult) when they go to public restrooms. Restrooms in malls, fast food restaurants, and highway rest areas have become places where people (including gang members) looking for trouble tend to hang out.

2. Make the buddy system a habit.

It is commonly known that if you practice something for 30 days it will become a habit. For one month structure or reinforce the use of the buddy system with your children. It will become a family habit before you know it.

16

Take The
Safe Route Home

"Children love to find the shortest way home: it makes them feel smart and powerful. Criminals often look for their victims in these out-of-the-way places."
– "How to Raise a Street Smart Kid," HBO

The safest route home from school, friends' homes, or anywhere children go regularly is the same route each time. This way children become familiar with the route and with the location of places where they can go for help along the way, such as a business or "safe house." Also, if your children take the same route home, you can accurately gauge the time it takes them. And if a child is ever missing, parents know exactly where the child may have been last, and they can backtrack on the route to search for the child.

ACTION STEPS

1. If your children walk home from school, instruct them to take the same route home every day.

They should never take shortcuts. Walk the route with them and plot out where they would run to if they are ever scared. Look for public places such as convenience stores and "safe houses," and for pay-phones along the route.

2. Instruct your children to go directly to their destination after school.

Whether they are going home, to a baby-sitter's house, to a neighbor's home, or to the library, children should go directly to that location. Make it a rule that your children must get your permission to take a different route home, for any reason.

3. Teach your children to avoid unknown routes.

If, for any reason, they do end up on an unknown route home, they definitely should not go down alleys, side streets, or walk through empty lots. They should instead stick to heavily trafficked streets and walk purposefully down the middle of the sidewalk.

4. Instruct your children to go to a place of business or a "safe house" if they are ever scared.

If they are ever approached by a stranger on the way home or if they ever feel that someone may be following them, children need to know where they should go to find safety. To be sure they understand this safety rule, play "what-if" games. For example, ask them where they would go if a man in a car slowed down near them while they were walking home.

5. Instruct children to sit near the bus driver or near a mother with children if they have to ride public transportation.

They should stay aware of the people who are sitting around them.

17

Walk Tall!

"Teach your kid to be alert."
– "Better Safe Than Sorry," <u>Starweek</u>

So if your parents get lost
It's your turn to be the boss
I'll be walkin' real tall
And in no time at all
They'll be laughin' and cryin'
They showed up in no time

"If Your Parents Get Lost" from *Can't Fool Me!*
Yello Dino Records

Children who look like they are not paying attention or look easy to scare are the easiest for abductors to manipulate and overpower. Children should stay alert to avert danger. Parents should teach children to walk tall and with confidence – even if they are scared and don't feel confident. Acting confident can be very useful when it comes to staying safe. Street safety includes walking purposefully, putting a bounce in your step, looking around you, and being alert "like a deer" to the people coming and going around you. Children should also not stroll on the streets or "hang out," especially streets with which they are not familiar. They should always look as though they have to be at a certain place at a specific time.

1. Practice walking purposefully with your child.

You can help them understand this concept by showing them how to "walk tall." They should look confident, alert, and unafraid. They should also stay alert to the world around them, for example, the people near them and the part of town they are in. It is important not to overcompensate, however; in other words, they should not try to look like they are *looking* for trouble or they may attract a bully. Also, if a child feels frightened for any reason, they should try to calm down and keep their focus on using their personal safety skills to get home safely.

18
Use A "Code Word"

"A man who tried to abduct a 9-year-old Tacoma-area girl got nowhere this week when he could not supply the 'password.'"
   – A letter writer to "Dear Abby"

Banana Man! Blue Sugar! Mary Poppins! Those are just a few examples of "secret" code words. Every family has emergencies at one time or another, so parents should prepare their children with a plan of action before this occurs. One part of this action plan should be code words for your children. A code word can help to ensure that your children will not accept a ride with any adult whom you have not approved, not even a friend of the family.

Imagine this scenario: a pleasant looking man approaches your child at school and says, "Hello, I work with your mother. She wasn't feeling well so we took her to the hospital. She told me to pick you up and take you to her." What is a child to think? Should she go? After all, her mother is sick. Emergency lures such as this one have been used by many child abductors. Many children have been saved from this ploy because their family had planned ahead.

There is strong controversy over the value of code words among professionals in this area. A code word can be a good idea for some families. However, some abductors are so clever and charming that they can get children to tell them their code words. Each parent has to determine if the code word will be an effective safety tool for their children.

Can your child keep a secret? Is he easily charmed by engaging adults? Or is he cautious around people he does not know?

> *What if a person tells you that*
> *Your family's hurt and down*
> *What do you do when they say come*
> *And no one can be found*
>
> *"What's my code?"*
> *"Hey, what's my code?"*
> *That's how you can begin*
> *If they don't know*
> *Take three steps back*
> *Then run like the wind*

"Tricky People" from *Can't Fool Me!*
Yello Dino Records

To be effective, your child cannot tell anyone their code word. It has to be a secret between you and your child. If a person does try to pickup your child but doesn't know the code word, your child must understand that guessing is not allowed; either the person knows the code word or he does not.

ACTION STEPS

1. Have your child pick a "secret" code word that only you and your child know.

In most families, every child should have his own

code word. However, some families may want just one "family" code word. If anyone, even a family acquaintance, approaches your child and says something like, "Your mother told me to pick you up after school," instruct your child to ask for the code word. If the person does not know it, then your child knows that you did not authorize this person to pick them up. If this ever occurs, instruct your child to leave immediately or to "take three steps back" and "run like the wind!"

2. Do not pick an obvious code word.

Once you are comfortable that your child can easily keep a secret, together choose a code word. Remember that if a person were to try and guess a child's code word, words such as "ninja," "pizza," or "ice cream" would be obvious guesses. So choose words or phrases that are out of the ordinary like "Easter eggs," or are personal to your family like the name of a place your family recently visited such as "Lake Burton." One expert advises parents to help children pick two contrasting words such as "purple tiger." The contrast gives you a phrase that is not logical enough for anyone to guess, and yet easy for your child to remember. Important: do not use the code word phrases provided as examples in this book.

3. Instruct your child not to tell anyone the code word.

Explain to your child why you need a code word and when you will use it. Tell them that occasionally there may be times when you cannot get to school to pick them up. On those days you may have to send someone else. To be absolutely sure that it's someone you want your child to go with, they should know the code word.

4. Create a new code word if yours is used or accidentally revealed.

If your child does give out their code word accidentally, or if they ever have to use it, then you should create a new code word.

5. Remind each other from time to time what your code word is.

Since it will be the rare occasion that you will ever actually need to use a code word, every so often you and your child should remind each other what your code word is.

19
Follow Your
Lost and Found Plan

I'm awalkin' through the mall
I'm awalkin' real tall
I'm findin' help right here
I'll betcha mom's real scared
Mom's probably just runnin' behind
She'll do better next time

"If Your Parents Get Lost" from *Can't Fool Me!*
Yello Dino Records

Before your child ever gets lost and has to face this fright-ening situation alone, teach him what to do and how to get help. If a child is separated from you or lost, he will often freeze because he is not sure where to go or what to do. A child who is not prepared to handle himself if he is ever lost may have visions of "strangers" lurking

behind every corner. This is self-defeating. He needs to be calm so that he can focus on staying safe and getting found. A child with a "lost and found" plan will be less scared and, therefore, less likely to find himself in greater trouble.

ACTION STEPS

1. Prepare your children with a plan before they are ever lost.

Tell your children that if they are lost in a public place, they should stay calm and alert. A child's natural response when lost is to wander around, which must be avoided. Generally, they should stay within the area that they last saw you. They should keep their eyes open for someone who can help them, such as a police officer, store clerk, bus driver, or a mother or grandmother with children. Your child should approach that person and tell him or her that he is lost. Then he should give the person his name, his parents' names, and ask the person to page his parents over the loud speaker, if available. If appropriate, the child can give his address and telephone number to the person helping him.

2. Instruct your children to never leave a public area to look for you.

If they are ever lost they should never go into an area where they could get into greater trouble such as a parking lot, dark hallway, or alley. They should stay within the public area and not leave the store or go to the back office of the store with anyone.

3. Plan ahead when on an outing.

When you are out in a public place with your children, such as in a mall or theme park, agree beforehand on a meeting spot in case you get separated. For example, agree to meet at a bench near a fountain or in front of a particular store. You should instruct very young children to stay near the spot where they last saw you; tell them you will backtrack your steps to find them.

4. Regularly review with your children what they should do if they are ever lost.

They will need reminders as they grow up. Test their comprehension of their "lost and found" plan by having them describe it to you.

5. Tell your children that if they are ever lost or taken you will look for them until they are found.

Children will feel more confident and less scared knowing that you will be looking for them if they are ever lost.

20

Go To The Right
Strangers For Help

I can find a mom with kids
I'll be glad if I did
Ah! a security guard
That wasn't very hard
Dad's probably just runnin' behind
He'll do better next time

"If Your Parents Get Lost" from *Can't Fool Me!*
Yello Dino Records

"Teaching children to avoid all strangers isn't useful . . .
If children develop a fear of strangers, you're setting
up a dangerous situation . . . If they're ever alone and
in trouble, they're isolated from help."
– "Careful, Not Fearful," <u>Sesame Street Parents' Guide</u>

Telling your child to "never talk to strangers" without
qualifying this rule is setting your child up for trouble.
If they ever become lost, they may not know what to do.
Remember that a child approaching a stranger for help and
a stranger approaching a child are two very different things.

Parents should explain to their children that there are
times when they do have to approach strangers. For example, if they are lost it is smart for them to go to a stranger
for help – it just has to be the right kind of stranger. The
right "strangers" might include a mother with children, a
grandmother, a store clerk, a security officer, a policeman,
etc. The following true story from Debi Fuller, a Dolton,
Illinois mother, shows that going to the right person, in this
case a security guard, can help:

"On a family outing to the ballpark, our eight-year-old daughter became separated from us as we were trying to exit the stadium. Our first reaction was to panic. How were we going to find her in a crowd of 47,000 people? A security guard saw the frightened look on our faces and asked if he could help. We explained the situation and showed him our SAFE-T-CHILD I.D. card. He smiled and told us that he had just seen a very scared looking child that looked just like her standing at the bottom of the exit ramp with another security officer – they were looking for her family. Within seconds we were reunited with our daughter."

This little girl went to the right "stranger" for help.

ACTION STEPS

1. Teach your children which strangers to approach for help.

If they need help in a public place, teach them to approach, for example, a policeman, a security guard, a lifeguard, or a mother with children.

2. Instruct your children to never leave a public area with the stranger they have approached for help.

If the adult says, "Come with me to the office," and tries to take them anywhere, instruct your child to tell them, "My parents told me to wait right here."

21

Follow Home Alone Safety Rules

"While it's sometimes necessary for an 8- or 9-year-old to be home alone, the data show that it's a frightening experience for them. Be sure the child knows how to lock and unlock the doors and what to do if a stranger calls or knocks on the door. Give them phone numbers of people to call if there's any problem, and give them strategies to cope, rather than just saying, 'This is good practice for you.'"

– "How Parents Can Talk to Their Kids," <u>Newsweek</u>

Children need to know what to do if they are ever home alone. Even if you think that you never leave your children alone, there are times when you do. For example, when you are in the shower, in the garden, or taking a nap, they are on their own. When your child is alone at home, he will be the only one available to answer the door or telephone. So he should know exactly how to handle these situations. It is critical that he does not give any specific information over the phone such as his name, your name, your address, and, of course, saying that he is home alone. Establish concrete guidelines for your children when they are by themselves at home. Prepare them so that they feel confident if anything ever happens.

Action Steps

1. Tell your children to never tell anyone that they are home alone.

In fact, they should not give any information to a phone caller or a person at the door. You may want to instruct your children to let your answering machine screen all phone calls. If someone does reach them over the telephone or knocks on the door, your children should tell the person that their parent or guardian is busy and will call them back when they are available. Or, since this line is so commonly used, you could prepare a statement that is more specific and also logical to your family. For example, if you garden regularly, your children could tell callers you are busy in the garden. Or if you nap in the afternoon, your children could inform callers you are napping and will call them back. Your children should not be persuaded to open the door for anyone who has not been approved, such as a person delivering flowers, a repair man, a neighbor, anyone in a uniform (even a police officer), or someone who says there is an emergency and they need to use the phone.

2. Practice the "home alone" skills.

When your children are home alone, check on their skills by calling them and knocking on the door. Have them practice saying things like, "My mother is taking a nap. She'll call you back." To further clarify this in

108

your children's minds, practice "what-if" situations. Ask your children, for example, "What if a policeman came to the door and said there was an accident or other emergency in the neighborhood and they had to open the door?" Let your children answer; if necessary, help them to find the right response. In this situation they could tell the officer that they will call the police department for confirmation before opening the door.

3. Make sure your children know who to call in an emergency.

Keep all important phone numbers such as trustworthy neighbors and your work number in a convenient place. Also review when to call "911" or "0" for operator in your area.

4. Make sure children five years of age and older know how to lock and unlock all of your doors and windows.

They should also know how to work the alarm system if you have one.

5. Review other "home alone" emergency plans, such as what to do in case of a fire.

Many safety-related organizations such as local fire departments, provide this type of information. Be sure to keep all emergency telephone numbers near your telephone, including the phone number for the local hospital and the poison control center.

109

22
Never Leave Your
Young Child Unattended

"If one mother will listen and realize that all it takes is
a second. Go in and answer the phone, go in and grab
a Pepsi out of the refrigerator . . . You come back out
and your kid ain't going to be there."
> – Mother of three-year old, who was abducted and mur-
> dered, "Kids and Strangers," WKRC-TV 12,
> Cincinnati

From *The Oprah Winfrey Show* to *Time* magazine, the
message is clear: don't turn your back or you may lose
the most precious gift you have. One of the themes of several talk and news magazine shows has been the speed with
which a child abductor can lure children out of parks or
even out of their own yards. In most cases during the sim-
ulated abductions, the actors could lure the children out of
their parents' sight in under one minute!

Most parents feel they keep a close eye on their children, and they don't often worry about someone walking
off with them. Yet there is case after case where parents have
turned their back for ten minutes, five minutes, and even
one minute and their child was gone. In some instances,
the abduction was described as occurring right under the
parent's nose. There is the case of six-year-old Melissa Lee
Brannen, who was taken from a neighborhood Christmas
party while her mother turned to get her coat and hug a
friend good-bye. Five-year-old Michael Dunahee was playing on a playground; when his parents returned five minutes later he was gone. In Plano, Texas, seven-year-old

Ashley Estell went to the playground while her brother played soccer for just a few minutes, she was abducted and killed.

What is a parent to do? How can they keep their eye on their children every second of every day? Clearly, they cannot. But parents have to be cautious so that they can reduce the odds that their children will ever be harmed. To start with, until children are about age three, parents should be vigilant about not letting them out of their sight. Also, since children that young can't tell the difference between a good and bad stranger, parents have to teach them not to wander off when they're in a crowd or public place. If children tend to wander off too much, reconsider going to the ball game or find a baby-sitter.

Parents should realize that if they are with their children at a playground or public pool, for example, they must <u>be</u> with them. If they are talking to another adult, their child is technically on their own. Remember, police and martial arts experts say that if your child is just 21 feet away from you they could get into danger and you would not necessarily be able to help them.

ACTION STEPS

1. Do not let children under three years old out of your sight.

Also teach young children not to wander off in crowds and public places.

111

2. Teach children that they must not run away from you.

Some small children are amazingly fast, and since they are so small, they can easily get lost in a crowd. They should be taught that they must never run away, in fact, they should always stay close by your side.

3. Never threaten to abandon your children.

It's easy to become tired or frustrated with a slow-moving or temperamental child when in a public place such as a mall. However, threatening to leave them and walking away is clearly not a safe way to handle the situation. Instead, carry the child or place him in a stroller.

23
Teach Your Child
The Correct Vocabulary

"Show me a kid that knows nothing about sex and I'll show you my next victim."
— NBC's *The Crusaders*

"If they don't have the vocabulary to talk about their body parts, then if something happens they can't tell anybody. They know that it's off-limits to talk about. They can't get help."
— Dr. Ian Russ, Ph.D, ABC's *The Home Show*

Caring parents are the best first teachers of any information that leads to children's sexual education. One of the first steps is to give them the names of their private parts. Private parts include the genital area, the buttocks, and the breasts — essentially the area covered by their underwear and bathing suits. If parents are uncomfortable with the clinical names they should use the phrase "private parts." Children should feel as comfortable telling you if someone is abusing them as they would telling you about a scraped knee. It's only when they feel comfortable naming body parts that they can distinguish good touches from bad touches and tell you about it.

Most children can't identify their body parts or they find it too embarrassing. But young children can be taught to speak openly and naturally about their bodies. By learning the names of the body parts instead of the slang terms, children receive a subtle message that their genitalia and those of others are important and worthy of discussion in a language of respect.

113

ACTION STEPS

1. Give your children names for their private parts.

At the age of two or three, while children are learning names for their body parts such as toes and fingers, they are receptive, curious, and open. This is the time to introduce words such as penis and vagina. If this subject is too uncomfortable for you to deal with, consider obtaining one of the many children's educational books to assist you.

24

Follow House And
Car Safety Rules

"It's believed that Polly Klaas's killer came in through
an unlocked back door."
  – "Child Abductions: What a Mom Must Know,"
  McCall's

S ometimes the obvious things are overlooked for the sake
of convenience, such as leaving a sleeping child in the
car for a few minutes while you run into a store. Often,
child abductors are looking for just such an opportunity. In
an example that terrified parents across the country, Polly
Klaas's abductor and murderer is believed to have gone
right through an open window or door in the house. For
this reason, parents in small towns can no longer assume
that they do not have to follow the same safety rules as parents who live in the city. As we've seen on television, our
mobile society makes every house in every city and town a
potential target. Appropriate safety guidelines must be considered in every home.

For added safety, the local police in many communities
will meet with groups of families to describe how they can
keep their homes safer and they will often even help set up
"block watch" programs. It never hurts to have your neighbors watching out for your safety and you watching out for
theirs, in fact, police say these are some of the safest neighborhoods.

ACTION STEPS

1. Lock the doors and windows of your home; be sure you have good locks, such as dead-bolts.

2. Be sure your house has good lighting.

All entries should have lights that can be turned on from inside the house. Flood lights allow you to look into your yard at night if you hear any noises.

3. If necessary, install an alarm system in your home.

Some neighborhoods are more susceptible than others, so many families have home alarm systems.

4. Provide easy access to telephones from every room.

You may want to install child monitors in the bedrooms of younger children.

5. Never leave children in the car while you run an errand – even for a minute.

6. Help to set up an organized "block watch" program in your neighborhood.

Contact your local police department for more information.

25

Establish School Safety Rules

"Check and see if your school has a call-back program. That's one thing you can do today . . . Make sure the schools in your area at least inform the parents if the students do not attend school. That's one little step you can do today."
– Oprah Winfrey, NBC's *The Oprah Winfrey Show*

Children spend much of their time at school. Not coincidentally, schools are a place where child molesters and abductors look for children. In some instances abductors target a child in the morning as the child is walking to school, then take them in the afternoon while the child is walking home. There are also documented cases of abductors posing as friends of the family to pick children up after school. Parents need to be vigilant to ensure that their children's schools are ensuring your children's safety with active policies such as call-back programs and specific pick-up instructions.

ACTION STEPS

1. Establish firm school pick-up permission.

Make sure that your school and daycare center will not give your child to anyone without your specific written instructions. Child I.D. cards, which identify the correct parent or guardian, can be especially good for this purpose.

2. Require immediate notification if a child is absent from school.

Insist that your children's schools and daycare centers offer a program that notifies parents immediately if a child is absent. If necessary, help set up a call-back program in your children's schools. If one of your children is absent, a school official should call you at home or at work, to confirm your child's where-abouts. That way, if your child is missing, a search can begin immediately and precious hours won't be lost.

26
Know The People
In Your Child's Life

It is amazing the number of incidents of child abuse where the children had been spending time with the adults for a long time, and the parents never even knew the people. Molesters gravitate toward children. They often look for jobs or volunteer opportunities where they will be in close proximity to large numbers of children. Parents cannot automatically assume that every coach, every scout leader, and every neighbor is a person with whom they should let their children be alone.

It deserves repeating. Child molesters nearly always look like "nice guys." On the surface they can be very kind, charming people. But there are uncountable stories about how large numbers of children are molested by people their parents thought were safe. One convicted molester says that within a week of meeting him, one set of parents let him baby-sit their children, one of whom he molested. He says that because he was a youth group supervisor and looked clean-cut, they blindly trusted him with their child. Remember, child molesters often cloak themselves behind a mask of being a "good Samaritan" type person.

The only way to keep children safe is to check out the

people they spend time with. In particular, parents should be alert if another adult shows their child a great deal of attention. There must be some reason why. As Major Calvin Jackson, a leading forensics expert and child abuse investigator, has said, "If an adult likes spending more time with your child than you do, the chances are you have a problem. Parents should become suspicious of these individuals and become vigilant."

However, to protect their children, parents do not have to go overboard; the majority of the people working with children are devoted professionals who simply love working with children. Parents just have to be smart. If something seems "fishy" it just might be. Just as children need to trust their instincts, parents also need to do the same.

This safety rule boils down to one simple guideline: don't accept new people into your child's life blindly. This also means that parents should get to know their child's friends and the parents of their friends. And they should communicate with their child and find out who they are spending time with. Parents should also be aware that many molesters, after being "discovered" in one community, will move to another community.

ACTION STEPS

1. Be involved in your children's activities and know your children's friends.

Check out their friends' homes and meet their parents before letting them sleep over or go on any outings. Keep track of their names, addresses, and telephone numbers. If your child likes spending a lot of time at any particular friend's or neighbor's home, drop in from time to time unexpectedly to check on them and see what they are up to. Also be wary of adults who display an inappropriate level of interest in your child – such as taking them shopping or showering them with gifts.

2. Communicate with your children.

Ask them who they spend time with, what those people are like, and what they do when they are together. Listen and watch carefully for anything that sounds out of the ordinary. Watch your child's behavior after he has spent time with a new friend, whether it's a peer or an adult. If his personality starts changing with that person's influence, you may want to find out why.

3. Do not base your trust of people on superficial appearances.

Remain aware of the potential for abuse. Outside their friends, thoroughly check out the people your children spend time with. Ask for references from baby-sitters, daycare operators, and other adults with whom you will place your children's care. Also ask for references from any adult who will be supervising your child away from school grounds, such as a coach, scout leader, or youth group leader. Check out those references or network with parents who have. Be particularly alert to an adult who is new in town. Find out if the person knows anyone locally who can vouch for them.

121

27

Don't Advertise
Your Child's Name

"Don't put your child's name, first or last, visibly on
hats, caps, jackets, bikes, wagons, etc. Remember, a
child responds to a first name. A person using that
name will automatically not be thought of as a
stranger."
— "Prevention Tips for All Ages," <u>Missing Children
Report</u>

Putting your children's names on the outside of their
clothing or other personal possessions gives abductors
an inside track, because children can be disarmed by a person calling them by name. If a person calls your child by
name, your child may believe that this person knows them
or knows their parents, and they will believe that it is okay
to go with that person. However, proper identification on
your child is important. It just needs to be concealed, for
example, on I.D. jewelry or on an I.D. card they carry in
their pocket or purse.

ACTION STEPS

1. Make sure your children's names do not appear prominently on any of their possessions such as clothes, bicycles, or school books.

If you want them to wear an I.D. bracelet or other identifying item, be sure their name is not easily visible. For example, on the I.D. bracelet the name could be engraved on the inside. On most I.D. jewelry engraving is small and hard to read unless held properly under the light, so these are generally fine.

28

Carry Proper I.D.–
It's Critical!

"You'd be surprised how many times we go to a parent and ask them, 'give us a good picture of your child so we can get it on the news or we can get it distributed out,' and they don't have a clear picture, the child is not by himself, and it's not recent. Sometimes as much as five years old, and on an eight year old that's a lot of difference. They need to have current pictures of these kids."

> – Sgt. Judy ., Dallas Police Dept., *Spectrum*, Channel 5 News

"'There are so many families that don't even have pictures of their kids, much less recent ones. They don't have their exact height or weight measurements. You've got to think about keeping things like that,' said Detective Larry Hanna, another investigator in the missing persons unit."

> – "Parents Warned to be Prepared," <u>Las Vegas Review-Journal/Sun</u>

Proper child I.D. works. So, parents and guardians should carry an I.D. card for each one of their children in their wallets. Then if you think that your child is missing or lost, you can respond immediately by handing the I.D. card over to authorities on the spot. This speeds up the search for the lost child immeasurably. Authorities agree that the faster you act, the faster you'll find your child.

It is well documented by police that when a child is lost it is very difficult for emotionally distraught parents to think clearly and remember the correct actions to take. At a time like this, it is sometimes impossible for even loving parents to correctly describe their child, let alone remember the steps to take to find him. "He's about three feet tall. He has blond hair . . . no, well . . . it used to be blond . . . it's more toward light brown now . . ." Imagine how many little boys or girls might fit a verbal description of your child in a mall on a Saturday afternoon! The following story illustrates this point:

> "I was feeling very stressed and had a real fear of not knowing what happened to my daughter, and these feelings made it hard to remember and to relay to the police many of her important characteristics. Angela's SAFE-T-CHILD I.D. card helped speak for me because it contained all her vital information and special identifying features. With the help of the I.D. card, which I kept in my wallet, the police were able to help find my daughter quickly."
>
> – Parent, New Castle, DE

Moreover, when we are frightened or panicky our body jumps into the "fight or flight response." Large amounts of adrenaline are dumped into our bloodstream. Many of our functions slow down or even shut down so that we can focus on exactly what we need to do to respond to the emergency. In these situations, we tend to develop "tunnel vision," where we can lose sight of everything but the emergency at hand. In the case of a lost child all of our signals are shouting, "Find my child!" What parent wants to try and remember the proper emergency procedures, or to stand at a counter and struggle to identify his child to security officers at a time like this?

Proper child identification is critical at this moment. But what is proper child I.D.? Few parents know that answer and many security professionals have never really thought it through. Since showing concern for missing children gains media attention and reflects community concern, I.D.s are often used as promotional items. Offering the I.D. makes the sponsor look good, but too often little attention is given to the function, content, and quality of the I.D. As SAFE-T-CHILD has experienced many times, parents may at some time really need to use these I.D.s! That is why it's important to make sure that the I.D. card contains all of the necessary information in a format that is useful at the time of the crisis.

SAFE-T-CHILD has conducted extensive research over the years, including talking to law enforcement officials and investigators who work to find missing children, to establish what makes a child I.D. valuable. Three crucial points arose from the research: 1. the I.D. information must be with parents at the moment that their child is lost, that's why the laminated, wallet-sized I.D. cards are the best, 2. the I.D. card must contain the specific information that security or law enforcement officers need, presented in a specific format, and 3. the card should contain emergency instructions for the parent which help them do the right thing in a high-stress situation, when it is difficult to think clearly. Many child I.D. products are not complete and may give parents a false sense of security. Furthermore, most I.D. products are not true *immediate response* child I.D.s. Most, such as "passport" type I.D. kits or police home record files, are stored at home and, therefore, are generally only useful when a child is missing for a longer time.

To respond quickly to a missing child, law enforcement officers need the I.D. card to contain certain vital information. Most important is a color photograph of your child and your child's physical description. They also need your child's birth date, key physical identifiers, medical emergency information, and parent or guardian information. Surprisingly, the nickname can also be essential, because a child under seven will often not answer to his or her formal name when lost or under stress. A good fingerprint can also be helpful if you do not have a full set of fingerprints filed at home.

In some cases, parents like to provide their children with proper I.D. to carry on school field trips or other group outings. If they are lost, injured, or become ill while away from home, law enforcement or security officers will have key information to help them. However, when children carry an I.D. the identifying information should never be visible or easily accessible to others. As previously mentioned, child abductors have been known to use information such as the child's name or address to gain access to them. If your child is going on a school trip or on an outing with friends, parents can pin an I.D. card to his or her shirt with the identifying information turned toward the inside. Children can also wear I.D. in the form of bracelets (with the identifying information on the inside), shoe tags, or necklaces.

For further information about I.D. cards and other child security products and services, see Appendix C.

ACTION STEPS

1. Carry a child I.D. card with correct information in your wallet at all times.

The SAFE-T-CHILD I.D. card is a good example of the information parents need to provide to authorities if one of their children is ever lost or missing. (See pictures in Appendix C.)

127

2. Provide your children with I.D. cards or other I.D. products.

These might be in the form of bracelets, shoe tags, or necklaces. Teenagers should also carry I.D. cards with them at all times. They not only provide identifying information, but may also include special emergency hotline telephone numbers if your child ever finds himself in trouble.

3. Make a mental note of what your children are wearing each day.

You should be able to accurately describe your child if they are ever lost or missing. What they are wearing could help distinguish them from the crowd.

29

Promote Your Child's Self-Esteem

"Once the child experiences the power to keep themselves safe, it affects other areas of their life. Self-esteem and confidence soar. We want to teach children that they have the right to be safe and to prevent them from becoming victims . . . Children who have had a sense of their power, and who have been taught to think for themselves, are the safest children of all."
 – "You've Got the POWER!" video, *Warrior Spirit*

"I believe it's time that everybody in America started treating their children differently . . . We have to make sure our children understand that they have self-esteem . . ."
 – Mark Klaas (Polly's father), *Donahue*

Strong self-esteem can be a child's best defense in staying safe. For one thing, children with self-esteem will have the confidence to perform all of the important safety rules that will help them keep themselves safe. Parents will be making a huge investment in their children's welfare by taking the time to promote self-esteem. Moreover, self-esteem will spill into other important areas of your children's welfare, such as avoiding youth violence and peer pressure to do drugs.

Often parents say that they hesitate to approach the topic of personal safety with their children for fear it will scare them and break down their self-confidence. But it's the way you as the parent handle this issue that determines how it is internalized by your child. Safety education should be a part of helping your children develop a realistic and balanced perspective of people and the world they live in as they grow.

A child's self-esteem comes from developing confidence in their abilities and skills. Many police and investigators feel the real value of martial arts classes is to help children's self-confidence grow. After all, it is unrealistic to expect a 60-pound child to fight it out with a 200-pound man. Instead, knowing they should cause a commotion, yell, resist, and then run to a safe place are some of a child's best defenses. Confident children do this best.

Building self-esteem in kids doesn't require that much time or effort. Surprisingly, simple things over time can work wonders. For example, including your child in the family's decision-making process, whether it is planning and cooking a meal or helping to plant a garden, shows that you respect their thoughts and opinions. Building self confidence can begin with little steps such as this example from my husband:

"The other day I was at Taco Bell and my young son wanted another tostada. I realized this would be a great opportunity to help build his confidence and comfort in speaking to an adult. I told him that he could go buy his tostada and that I would be watching. I gave him a dollar and off he went. After navigating through some cool teens, a frazzled mom, and a bored cashier, he pulled it off. He returned with the change, his tostada, and a big grin. It seems small, but it was very important to him. Little things like this accumulate to build self-esteem in a child."

ACTION STEPS

1. Find your children's qualities, verbalize them, and encourage them.

Also, identify their weaknesses and help them work through, improve, and accept them. While recognizing your children's unique qualities, pay attention to their strengths and weaknesses as they relate to personal safety. For example, you may have an extremely friendly child who loves to talk to people. That child will require extra knowledge regarding why she should not make friends with people she doesn't know until you also get to know those people.

2. Reinforce your love often.

Children need to know they are loved and believed, so it is important to reinforce your love frequently. Tell your children too that if they were ever lost you would never stop loving them or looking for them, ever.

3. Be aware of how you present safety education to your children.

Don't project your fears and don't be unnecessarily dramatic. Fear can damage self-esteem, and the confidence that springs from self-esteem underlies much of the safety rules. It can also be weakening, not empowering, to be too graphic about the consequences. After all, when you teach your child to look both ways before crossing the street you don't

131

describe the vivid detail of what happens if your child gets hit by a car.

4. Involve your children in adult activities.

For example, while shopping you can let them pay the cashier. This will develop their confidence in interacting with adults they do not know and help them learn to assert themselves in a "big person's" world.

5. Learn more about developing your child's self esteem.

There are hundreds of books on this topic. Visit your local library or bookstore to find a book that suits your taste.

30
Listen To
Your Child

"If you talk to your children and they talk to you, you establish an open relationship with your children *before* you need it, not afterwards."
    – J.J. Bittenbinder, "Street Smarts: Straight Talk for Kids, Teens & Parents," PBS

Experts have described child abductors and molesters as the best child psychologists. It is your job to put the odds in your child's favor. One of the reasons that communication between a parent and a child is important is that children are easily swayed by the negative conditioning of molesters. By assuring your child that you will listen to him gives the child an escape route. Your mind will then be the one the abductor or molester is up against, not your child's.

Major Calvin Jackson tells this true story, which he experienced during his many years as a child abuse investigator:

"In one dramatic case, the person molesting children was a prominent member of the medical community. Parents often used the fatherly physician to provide treatment for their children. During interviews of families having used the doctor, it was disclosed that most of the children did not like the physician, and in fact cried and resisted vehemently when told they would have to see him. Parents attributed the fear to a general dislike for doctors, although some children informed the parents they did not like 'what' the doctor did to them. The parents never asked 'what' it was he did. In several instances the children described how he 'examined' them, requiring them to remove their garments, when in fact he was supposed to only check for minor ailments. Further, the parents did not make a distinction between their children's behavior when they visited other physicians and when they visited the molesting physician. The children did not resist being treated by other physicians. The unfortunate bottom line to this situation is that there were one hundred and twenty-three verifiable instances of sexual child molestation raised against the doctor at the time of his conviction."

This story is a classic example of parents not listening to their children and, when they do listen, of not really <u>hearing</u> their child. Unfortunately, this is among the most common mistakes parents make. With the present pace and demands of modern life, it is difficult for parents to even cover the basics for their families, let alone every detail. We all want to be the best parents we can possibly be. But as we rush from one responsibility to the next, our time with our children often comes down to just moments each day. In that short time, we mostly just cover the day-to-day basics. For example, an after-school greeting might go a lot like this: "Did your day go well at school? Did you have a snack yet? You look tired. You better try and go to bed earlier tonight. Did that cough bother you at school today? Do you have homework? You left your bed unmade this morning and you need to tidy up your room before you go out to play. Could you also help me bring in the groceries? Your father is working late tonight. I have to go pick up your brother. He's at his friend's house." This is not a likely time for deep communication, is it?

We listen to our children "on the fly," so to speak. This limits our capability to hear subtle fluctuations in their voices and to let things settle and see what is behind seemingly simple statements. Parents need to find the time of day that works best for them, whether it's right after school, during dinner, or just before bed.

Listening to our children often means stepping outside of our own inner world and our own problems, and really focusing on our children. We have all experienced that satisfied expression on our children's faces when we give them our full attention. There is no doubt that they feel special. We naturally give the courtesy of paying attention to adults when they speak, but it is often a courtesy we do not extend to our own children. Clinical psychologist Lawrence Kutner, Ph.D., believes that talking "with" our children is different from talking "to" them. In his book, *Parent and Child*, he acknowledges, "Communicating effectively with a child often requires that a parent combine the deductive skills of Sherlock Holmes with the boundless tact and patience of an ambassador." So, if at first you don't succeed, give your child repeated chances to express opinions, fears, or hopes.

Listening to your children may one day mean having to hear something that you find difficult. A child being molested or bothered may not speak about it directly. For example, your child may say to you, "Uncle John smells bad." If you were to respond, "That's not a nice thing to say about your father's brother," your child may take it to mean that you don't care and won't really listen if she were to tell you that Uncle John is coming into her room at night and fondling her. A simple response like, "What do you mean he smells bad?" might lead you in unexpected directions.

This open, loving relationship between parent and child has to begin early in life. Children must be raised with a strong sense that we will always love them and listen openly to them even when they do something bad. Be sure to let them know that while you may not like their action or behavior, you still love them. Your child also needs to know that your ears will be open to them even if an adult disagrees or counters them.

Loved. Nurtured. Believed. Empowered. These are the four pillars that will provide your child with the inner strength they need to stay safe. We need confident children, children who can be alone and take care of themselves – especially in today's uncertain world. By talking with and listening to your children, you will establish open communication and a sense of trust. This will encourage your child to discuss inner feelings and confide in you, and will set a pattern that will carry you both successfully into the future.

ACTION STEPS

1. Always try to listen to your children.

And try to figure out what they may really be saying. Remember that "Uncle Bill smells bad" may mean something else.

2. Even if they are misbehaving, your love should still be communicated.

Let them know that while you do not like their behavior and wish they would stop, it doesn't mean you don't love them.

3. Establish a line of communication with your children.

Talk frankly with them about the people in the world who might bother them. Child education experts say that you have to tell your 10-year-old what you want your teenager to know.

136

4. Never belittle their fears.

Our children are individuals – part of us, yet uniquely their own. They may have fears that we see as unrealistic. That doesn't mean that we should say things such as, "Oh, that's nothing to be afraid of." Instead, we should talk with them about their fears, giving them room to express those fears and offering them a wider perspective for them to understand why their fears don't have to be so scary.

5. Talk and discuss family issues at regular times.

Set up specific periods of time, such as after dinner, when every member of the family tells about their day or discusses things that are bothering them.

6. Give your children support when they make mistakes.

All children will make mistakes, such as forgetting to get your permission when they go to a friend's house one afternoon. You should assure your children that even if you are annoyed with them for the mistake, you still love them. And when your children are honest about their mistakes it can be reinforcing to show them that you appreciate their honesty by, for example, cutting back on their punishment.

7. Seek assistance from others.

As much as you might want to, you may not be available for your child at the exact moment they need you. This is why you should ensure that your children always have people in their lives in addition to you to whom they can talk. Choose those people carefully, whether it's a family member, friend, teacher, or childcare provider. This idea of building a family network to raise children is not new. In fact, an old African proverb says, "It takes a village to raise a child."

137

CHECK LIST

30 Simple Ways To Help Prevent Your Child From Becoming Lost, Missing, Abducted, or Abused

A Quick Review

✓ Child Tips

☐ **I. You Can Say "No!"** A child who can say "no" to an adult when he is uncomfortable or scared will be the child who has a chance to keep himself safe.

☐ **2. Identify Strangers.** Because children cannot tell from the outside if a person is bad or not, they needs to stay away from any person they do not know.

☐ **3. Beware of Tricky People.** To keep your children safe from the adults who prey on children, teach them more than just, "Don't take candy from strangers."

☐ **4. Cut The Dialogue!** Children have one strong power which will allow them to stop the powerful lures in their tracks – cut the dialogue!

☐ **5. My Body's Mine!** Children should understand that their body is theirs, and that means that they choose the level of physical affection that feels comfortable.

☐ **6. Trust Your Instincts.** One of the most important things to keeping children strong and free is for them to understand they should get help if something feels bad on the inside.

☐ **7. Take Three Steps Back.** Children should learn to stay at least three arm lengths away from any adult they do not know.

☐ **8. Yell! Yell! Yell!** Children can use their natural talent for yelling to protect themselves.

☐ **9. Run Like The Wind.** Children should know that to run from a suspicious stranger is the right thing to do.

☐ **10. Break Away!** While children cannot "beat up" an adult, in some situations they should put up a struggle if they are ever grabbed.

☐ **11. Tell Until Someone Listens.** Children should be given the power to tell a parent or someone they trust whenever they have a problem.

☐ **12. Don't Keep Bad Secrets.** Children should not keep secrets from parents or guardians.

☐ **13. Always Ask First.** Children should always tell a parent or caregiver before going anywhere.

☐ **14. Use The Telephone.** Children should know their telephone numbers, including area code; how to use various telephones; and when and how to dial "911" and "0."

☐ **15. Always Have a Buddy.** Children should always have a buddy when walking to school or in public places.

☐ **16. Take The Safe Route Home.** Children should always take the same route home from school and from friends' homes everyday.

☐ **17. Walk Tall!** Children should walk purposefully and stay alert.

☐ **18. Use a "Code Word."** Pick a code word with your child and use it carefully.

☐ **19. Follow Your Lost and Found Plan.** Children need to know what to do and how to get help if they are ever lost.

☐ **20. Go To The Right Strangers For Help.** Children should know what kind of strangers to go to for help if they are ever lost or in trouble.

☐ **21. Follow Home Alone Safety Rules.** Children need to know how to behave when they are home alone.

✓ <u>Parent Tips</u>

☐ **22. Never Leave Your Young Child Unattended.** Children under three years old are too young to be on their own.

☐ **23. Teach Your Child The Correct Vocabulary.** Children should know the names of their private parts.

☐ **24. Follow House And Car Safety Rules.**

☐ **25. Establish School Safety Rules.** Ensure your children's schools follow proper safety guidelines.

☐ **26. Know The People In Your Child's Life.** Be involved in your children's activities and know their friends.

☐ **27. Don't Advertise Your Child's Name.** Do not put your children's names visibly on any personal items.

☐ **28. Carry Proper I.D. – It's Critical!** Carry a child I.D. card for each of your children at all times, and give one to other caregivers.

☐ **29. Promote Your Child's Self-Esteem.** Strong self-esteem can be a child's best defense for staying safe.

☐ **30. Listen To Your Child.** If you talk to your children and they talk to you, you establish an open relationship before you need it, not afterwards.

WHAT YOU NEED TO KNOW ABOUT

PARENTAL ABDUCTIONS

141

Parental
Abductions

". . . most parental kidnapping is not done out of love for the child. 'The majority of parental kidnapping is due to rage of the other parent and a desire for control . . . Parental kidnapping is not good for the child. It creates anxiety, fright, depression, difficulty with trust, and fear of new people.'"
  – "Abduction by Parents: The Unrecognized Crime," Parents

"Parental abduction is not an innocent crime. It is not safe. It is not harmless. The children suffer as they are uprooted again and again. They lose any sense of security and belonging. Inside they bleed with guilt and overpowering sadness. And the family left behind sits in agony, awaiting a call – the call that will lift the enormous burden of pain from their hearts."
  – "From Visitation to Abduction: A Family's Nightmare," Missing Children Report

"Although parental kidnapping may not sound as traumatic as abduction by a complete stranger, the impact is just as devastating. The loneliness and loss I felt were terrible."
  – "Welcome home, Brian," Ladies' Home Journal (by Deborah Wilson Runner, mother who was separated from her son by her ex-husband for 15 years)

M any people are surprised at just how prevalent abduction of children by their non-custodial parents is. In fact, most parents never suspect their ex-spouse would literally kidnap their own child. Yet in 1988, the U.S.

143

Department of Justice found that each year over 350,000 children are taken by non-custodial parents – often separating the children from their custodial parent for many years. By comparison, there are 3,500 to 4,500 abductions by strangers each year, and only 150 to 300 of these are considered long-term abductions.

Many of these kidnappings occur during the divorce process when the parents' feelings about each other are often hostile. When one parent is feeling rejected or angry, taking the child can be seen as a way to get revenge or to punish the other parent. Whether based on anger, spite, or misunderstanding, if one parent decides to keep a child from the other parent, it can be done. And once abducted, the custodial parent must spend countless hours and thousands of dollars, not to mention the extreme emotional cost, trying to recover a child – a process that can seem like trying to find a needle in a haystack. Prevention is by far the best bet.

Among the thousands of cases of kidnapping by non-custodial parents are the following examples:

> "'David's birthday was coming up the next week, so I agreed that he [her former husband, Ralph] could see him for the day. We arranged a pickup in a parking lot because I still did not want him to know where we lived. When I arrived with both kids in the car, he punched me and stole them.'"
>
> – When Parents Kidnap: The Families Behind the Headlines, Geoffrey L. Greif and Rebecca L. Hegar

"On July 9, 1992, the unimaginable became a devastating reality. Heidi Hodges' three children, Hans, Heather and Laurel Holmgren, were kidnapped by their non-custodial father, Neil Holmgren. Neil Holmgren was blessed with many advantages: intelligence, striking good looks, convincing charm. A man who had all of the ingredients to have the whole world within his grasp. Few would suspect his dark side –

144

the grainy, unpredictable paranoia, his explosive temper and violent obsession for vengeance against his estranged wife." (Note: Neil has been located and the children have been recovered, 1994)

> – "From Visitation to Abduction: A Family's Nightmare," <u>Missing Children Report</u>

"The judge granted me physical custody of Brian. Mike received liberal visitation rights, yet this still angered him so much that, on several occasions, he threatened to take our son away from me. Concerned, I reported the threats to the judge, but he said that nothing could be done unless Mike actually acted on his threats . . . A week after the divorce became final, Mike came to pick up Brian for the weekend. He didn't return on Sunday evening, and no one answered the phone at the rooming house where he was staying."

> – "Welcome home, Brian," <u>Ladies' Home Journal</u>

Because the child is with a parent, people often don't view this form of abduction as tragic. But the seriousness of parental abductions is tragically underestimated. For one thing, the kidnapping parent is rarely motivated by concern for the child. Most often, a non-custodial parental abduction is an act of revenge committed against the former spouse. There is no love for the child in this situation. Could anyone really think that a balanced, loving parent would rip their child away from their other parent, siblings, and family members? Psychological, emotional, and/or physical abuse are the prices paid by the child in virtually every case. Remember that parental kidnapping is an illegal action, so the child is basically living life on-the-run, always in hiding and never able to establish long-term relationships or roots. For children, the pain of this life includes:

• Suffering the loss of the parent and family members from whom they were taken,

• Moving often, commonly having their name changed, being kept out of school, forced to tell lies, and not being allowed to establish normal friendships with other children,

• Experiencing anxiety, depression, difficulty with trust, and fear of new people,

• Dealing with self-esteem problems due to being told that the other parent doesn't want them (as often happens).

Steps to Prevent Parental Abduction

"As a former private investigator, I have worked closely with hundreds of families involving domestic and custody disputes, and criminal child abduction. I remain convinced of one fundamental truth: the majority of acts of child abduction are preventable. In particular, with non-custodial parental abduction I was continually shocked at how many signs there were before the abduction actually took place. And yet, the parents took no steps to educate their children and protect them from this occurring. Without question, parents who educate themselves and their children with the basic safety knowledge are empowered to act responsively rather than react helplessly to child abduction."

– Dr. George R. Jones, a crisis intervention specialist, minister, SAFE-T-CHILD Director, and former private investigator; Lynchburg, Virginia

If a parent is ever in a situation that could even remotely lead to a parental abduction, they must become vigilant. Protecting your child from an ex-spouse who is intent on abduction is extremely difficult. Recognizing this up front should encourage you to maintain at least a civil, if not friendly, relationship with your ex-spouse.

To protect your children, your first step should be to create a family plan that would help you be reunited with your child if you ever become separated. One important aspect of this plan is to gently, but thoroughly, prepare your child for the possibility of being taken by their non-custodial parent. You can begin this process by explaining to your child that the anger between you and your ex-spouse is not their fault. Tell them an angry parent can make big mistakes. Be sure they know you would always love and want them with you even if the other parent tells them that you don't. Then let them know that they can always call you to be sure it is okay with you to go with the other parent. If the other spouse will not let them call you then they should know that something is very wrong. As a back-up plan, you can select people whom the children can trust, so that they have a source besides yourself to contact if they are in trouble or if they think their abducting parent is lying to them. If that happens, they must follow your family plan of action.

Here are eight important steps custodial parents should take to help prevent an abduction from occurring and, if an abduction does occur, to help ensure a speedy recovery:

1. **Work through custody issues first**, before the property settlement, rather than after. This helps prevent the anger over property issues to impact custody decisions. Also, if you and your ex-spouse are having problems act quickly to establish legal custody. In some states where no custody is established, a parent taking his/her child is not illegal. (Know the laws that apply to custody and jurisdiction in your state or the state where the divorce occurred.)

2. **Include special provisions in the custody decree** such as specifying the beginning and end dates of visits, requiring legal approval to take the child out of state, and requiring written consent to take the child from school.

3. **Keep child support and visitations as separate issues.** A frustrated parent might take a child in anger if visitation rights are withheld. Do not antagonize him/her by with-

147

holding visitations based on support payments alone.

4. Do not ignore any abduction threat. Document the threats by having a witness, by tape-recording the event, or by keeping a log with the date, time and detailed description of the scenario. (Some states require that you tell the other person that you will be recording a phone call.) Threats made to take your child should also be taken seriously. Notify police and give them copies of any restraining orders that are in effect against your ex-spouse. You may also request restricted locations for visitation rights if you can prove potential harm to your child. The potential abductor should be advised that taking a child is punishable by imprisonment, a fine, or both. Notify schools, baby-sitters, and friends of your concern; make sure teachers will not release your child to your ex-spouse if you have legal custody.

5. Be on the alert for sudden changes in your ex-spouse's life. Any changes, such as quitting a job or selling a home, may be preparation to run off. If you notice sudden changes in your ex-spouse's behavior, take appropriate precautions. Trust your intuition.

6. Maintain records on your ex-spouse, such as job information, phone numbers and addresses of friends and family, social security numbers, license plate number, auto description, hobbies, financial records, and credit card numbers. In most custodial kidnappings a close friend or relative of your ex-spouse knows where the child is.

7. Discuss the potential abduction problem with your child, calmly. As mentioned above, discuss this topic of parental abduction with your child just as you would any of the other personal safety rules. Make sure your children know that if they were ever taken it would be against your will. Reassure them that if they are taken you will look for them until you find them.

8. Contact proper authorities. Do not delay if you think your child has been taken by your ex-spouse – begin your search immediately. Make sure if your child is abducted, that the police take the right type of report and that your child is entered into the FBI's National Crime Information Center (NCIC) system right away (a warrant is not required). Call back to confirm that it has been done. Hire a family law attorney to work with you. An attorney who is not experienced in custody matters will cost you lost time, money, and possibly custody in the long run. Also, a national missing child non-profit organization can assist you without charge. Among the services it can provide is referrals to professionals and social services, which you can rely on if you need guidance. For assistance in the U.S.A. and Canada call The National Center for Missing & Exploited Children (NCMEC) at 1-800-843-5678. For more information on this topic, NCMEC has a 78-page handbook on the subject.

Note: This section was created, in part, from information published by the National Center For Missing & Exploited Children.

HOPE
FOR THE
FUTURE

Hope For
The Future

"We, the people, do not have to tolerate these kinds of horrendous acts against our children . . . It is so ridiculous that we continue to let this happen day after day, and year after year, and cry our hearts out and let our hearts bleed and say isn't this a shame. When are we going to make the decision that we as a civilized society do not have to allow this to happen to our children."
   – Oprah Winfrey NBC's, *The Oprah Winfrey Show*

"Not long ago, a woman vacationing in Cancun, Mexico, noticed a child standing alone on a beach. Suspicious, she took a picture of the child and thought nothing more of it–until she returned to her home in Oakland, CA, and spotted what looked like the child on one of those cards that ask 'Have You Seen Me?' Shocked, she compared the picture of the missing child on the card with the photo of the child she'd taken in Mexico. They matched, and she promptly called the National Center for Missing and Exploited Children (NCMEC). Soon after, the child was recovered and the abductor apprehended."
   – "Have You Seen Me?," <u>Law Enforcement Technology</u>

Your concern for your children's safety encouraged you to read this book. Your attention to this topic proves that you realize child abuse and abduction is not something that "could never happen to me." As much as we might like to believe otherwise, this is not an issue that is far removed from any of our lives. With the knowledge you have gained you can help keep your children safer. But what about your friends' and relatives' children? What about the children who live in your neighborhood? Who will protect them if their parents don't have this knowledge or don't have the time, inclination, or circumstances to teach their children properly?

Wouldn't it be nice if the knowledge and the solutions you have gained through reading this book could reach other children? To help stop the pain that so many children are enduring sometimes means reaching outside of our own home and family. It means truly _using_ the knowledge you have gained in this book. It means becoming an advocate for children everywhere.

A child advocate is, simply, a defender of children. It doesn't mean you have to spend your life petitioning Congress to change laws. Sometimes the small steps can mean the most. There are many small things adults can do to help children: these small things that can easily be worked into your busy life. For example, I don't just share my knowledge of child security with my own children, I also share it with their friends and with their friends' parents. One day, I saw the effect of this sharing in action. My two children and three of their friends were playing in the front yard when a man, whom none of them knew, pulled into the driveway. As he was getting out of his car, he said hello to the children. They were polite, but all kept their distance. In fact, my son and his friend were standing behind a wheelbarrow, and they stayed put as the man smiled at them and said that he was here to see me and their father. I was very relieved as I watched the children out the window – they were definitely following the "stay three steps back from strangers" rule, which I had gone over with each of them.

Sharing this knowledge is so important. As Oprah Winfrey stated so beautifully, "We do not have to put up with these kinds of horrendous acts against our children." For example, now that you know some of the signs of suspicious adult behavior, you can better evaluate the situation, and if necessary check things out or get authorities to look into the situation. We may wish to remain silent in certain situations, hoping that we are wrong about our suspicions or simply not wanting to get involved. But if we learn to speak up for children, they will learn to speak up for themselves. If one of our children comes to us with a problem, we have to listen and respond appropriately. If they tell us about a friend of theirs who is having a problem we need to speak up. If we notice a potentially dangerous situation around one of our children or another child we need to speak up. This may not always be a simple or easy step. But if each one of us becomes an advocate for the children in our life, whether they are our own children or those around us, child abuse and abduction will significantly decline.

I encourage all adults to share this book with other parents and concerned adults. You will be helping to break down the denial response and open the doors to a better future for all our children.

How can each of us make a difference in this very important area? How can we help make sure that each child has the right to experience the innocence and beauty of childhood? What more can we possibly do in our hectic lives? Here are a few very simple things, which, if every adult did, would make a big difference in many children's lives:

1. **Talk to an adult who may be displaying questionable behavior.** What you should be able to spot is behavior that is making your child or someone else's child uncomfortable. When talking about a perceived "situation" to another adult, it's important to stay calm and focused. Most adults do not realize that their behavior may be making a child uncomfortable, so they may respond defensively at

first. If you stay calm and are understanding, you will be better able to diffuse the situation and address it if it is, indeed, serious. You can obtain more information if you do not set off "alarms."

2. Check out suspicious situations or get an authority figure to assist. While we cannot interfere with parents who are disciplining their children in public, we can and should do something if a child is yelling, "This is not my dad!" while crying or physically struggling. If the situation is not that extreme, but something about the situation still seems amiss, you could monitor the situation from a distance. Then if the situation worsens, you could move closer and see how the child responds to your presence. If you really start to worry, you can call a security guard or police officer to decide further action.

3. Check out the adults who spend time with our children. While we do not want to inappropriately accuse adults of indecent behavior with children, we should, as stated earlier in this book, check out the people in our children's lives. This means asking for and following up with references from coaches, baby-sitters, troop leaders, and other youth leaders. And it means dropping in on daycare centers and our children's friends' houses at unscheduled times.

4. Help set up "safe houses" and safety programs in your area. If you are screened and fingerprinted by the police, your home can be designated a Safe House. By hanging a sign in your window, children will know that your home is a safe place to go if they are lost, frightened, or being bothered. Adults can also enroll in the Safe Corridor project and walk children home from school. If you do, take the responsibility seriously and be home during the hours when children need you. And be sure your school has a well-run call-back program if children are absent from school, an active system for releasing children to adults other than the parents, and a plan to keep children safe on the way to and from school.

5. Help strengthen the laws against child offenders in your state. If you are inclined to participate in legal and legislative matters and have the resources, you can learn how to work to change laws regarding children's safety. In particular, it is important to encourage laws to register offenders.

6. Help set up a child security and identification program in your community. Programs such as The SAFE-T-CHILD Program, set up in schools, daycare centers, churches, businesses, and civic organizations, have helped millions of children gain safety knowledge.

Children are our most precious resource. Protecting them is the responsibility of every adult, because it is our children to whom we are passing on our world. It is our children's right to feel empowered and strong. Only when they feel this inner strength can we change the patterns of mankind from weak and destructive to strong and productive.

I sincerely thank you for the time you've spent reading this book. There is hope for the future. I invite you, personally, to join me in making this a safer world for our children.

SECTION 5

APPENDICES

APPENDIX A

The Tricks Used By "Tricky People"

O ne of the hardest topics for parents to understand and comprehend is the variety of "methods" that child molesters and abductors use to get physically close to children. One of the primary reasons that this topic is difficult to confront is because the approaches used by adults who "seduce" children appear, to the untrained eye, as normal behavior. In order to help parents understand so that they can keep their children safe from these approaches, we have compiled the following list of 11 "methods and styles of seduction" commonly used by child abductors and molesters. (This list is an expansion of the list of lures cited in "Tricky People," Simple Way #3.)

The following list was taken from a book written by Seth L. Goldstein entitled *The Sexual Exploitation of Children*. This book is used by child abuse investigators across the country and is considered the foremost textbook on this topic. Goldstein gained much of his knowledge while working as a City Police Officer and Investigator for the Santa Clara and Napa County, California, District Attorney's Office, where he specialized in child abuse cases for 13 years. During his years in the field, he worked one-on-one with many children and their families to bring the molesters to trial. Goldstein was also one of the founding members on the Board of Directors of the National Center for Missing and Exploited Children.

Goldstein participated in the group that developed investigative techniques that have become the standard in the professional field. The training curriculum they developed is used by the U. S. Department of Justice. According to Goldstein, the following common characteristics of sexual exploitation have been drawn from the vast number of cases of sexual abuse that have occurred in this country.

As you'll see from the following list, child molesters are very clever. They have tried-and-true ways to get access to children and to disguise their inappropriate – and unlawful – activities from the eyes of caring adults. Basically, their approaches with children are similar to the persuasive sexual approaches adults use with other adults; however, children don't have the sophistication to understand what is happening. The fact is, the child molester pursues his prey with purpose, and will use any method that works. Goldstein makes a direct comparison between stalking prey and the seduction of children. "The offender, once he has targeted a child, will track down and methodically approach the child and begin to work on seducing him. All the while, performing actions that appear, on the surface, to be normal. When in actuality he is introducing the child to sexuality."

All parents and guardians of children should understand these methods and styles of seduction used by child molesters so that they can keep their eyes and ears open for inappropriate actions, and help to let children live their young lives free from a molester's desires.

Methods and Styles of Seduction*
from *The Sexual Exploitation of Children*
by Seth L. Goldstein, J.D.

Affection and Attention

For the most part, a child is seduced in the same way as one adult seduces another. The offender takes him places,

---

* *Copyright CRC Press, Inc., Boca Raton, FL; reproduced with permission of publisher.*

buys him things, impresses the child with his own personality, makes the child feel loved and indebted to the offender, then becomes physical with the child. It starts subtly, by
holding hands, an arm over the shoulder, hand in lap, grad-
uating to more explicit conduct.

Mislabeling the Activity

Another common method of seducing the child is to
misrepresent what the offender is actually doing. This
could be by tricking the child into performing a sex act or
by using a legitimate activity to achieve physical contact
with the child, from which the offender can derive sexual
gratification. In one case, a man who engaged in sexual
activities with 8-to-9-year-old boys liked to play a game
called "monster," in which he would wrestle with the boys
and touch their genitals and other areas. All of this was
accomplished without the child's knowing what was actually going on. From this kind of activity, the offender will
graduate to more blatant touching. After the child feels
more comfortable with the idea of the offender breaking
the barrier of "personal space," the offender will advance to
sexual play.

A common ploy to trick the child into an act is to tell
the child that what is being done is for a purpose other than
the real one. For example, a young child was seduced into
posing for photographers by being told that the offender
was making pictures for a publisher of books for medical
practitioners–the pictures were to assist doctors in teaching
others about sex.

Misrepresentation of Moral Values

Possessing little experience or knowledge, the child is
often easily convinced that what the offender wants is a
legitimate activity. It is easy to understand why children
acquiesce to the demands of the child molester, considering

the vast literature on sex with children and sex manuals that are on the market. These are often left out and available for children to "discover" by accident or are specifically shown to the child by the offender. In many cases, children have been shown films that are either sexually graphic or suggestive.

Slow/Subtle Exposure to the Concept of Sexual Activity

By constantly talking to the child about sexual activities in the presence of the child, the offender slowly indoctrinates the child into the world of sex.

Curiosity

Another style of seduction is the generation of curiosity on the part of the child. This is often done by leaving sexually oriented materials out and available to the children. The seduction includes the use of sexual aids . . . which are left in areas where children can find them. This leads to conversations about sexual matters.

Narcotics and Alcohol

The use of narcotics and alcohol by the child molester is commonplace. What better way to get a child to a place he wouldn't ordinarily go to than to provide him with something he can't ordinarily get? The use of alcohol is mostly limited to the older child; however, it is also a common denominator in some cases involving young children.

Misuse of Authority

This may take two forms. In the first, the offender takes advantage of his power, as in the following example. A Boy Scout leader told the children in his troop, while on several outings, to disrobe. Over a period of time he graduated from fondling them to orally copulating with them. Each time he told them not to tell anyone.

In the second type of misuse of authority, the offender takes advantage of a position of special trust and represents the activity as legitimate, using his authority, stature, and position to convince the child that what he wants is OK.

Rewards and Bribes

A very common style of seduction is the use of rewards. Sometimes the child is told in advance what he will receive if he cooperates with the offender. Other times the offender doesn't tell the child until after the act. Soon the child learns that by doing what the offender wants, he can have his own way. The reward may be as elaborate as a car or as simple as an ice cream cone, depending on the circumstances.

Children are easily lured into big money by promises to make them Hollywood stars. The hopes of grandeur, and comparisons made by the offender between the child and the child's idols such as Brooke Shields, often make them easy prey. Modern advertising is often shown to the child, especially advertising that accents the sexuality of young children, to convince the child of the propriety of the acts.

Blackmail

Once the child has been placed in a compromising situation–sexually or otherwise–the offender can obtain some control over the child by threatening exposure. The offender knows that the child feels guilty and is wrought by shame. The offender also knows that most children have very little self-esteem or confidence and they feel helpless in the situation they are in.

A deep concern of many children who have a close relationship with the offender is the fear of being taken away, out of the family situation. This threat may be expressed or implied by the offender or may be developed by the child with no direct threats being made.

Use of Pornography

Both child and adult pornography is often used by the child molester to seduce the child. In addition to misrepresenting moral standards, the pornography can be used to demonstrate the acts in which the offender wishes to engage. It may also be used to stimulate the child's interest in the depicted activities and lower the child's inhibitions.

Threats

Rarely is a threat of harm used to get the child to comply with the act. The only time a threat becomes necessary is to keep the child quiet and to continue participating in what the offender desires. For the most part, threats are made that imply negative consequences for both the victim and the offender if there is disclosure.

New Child Abuse Service Serves as Advocate to Parents and Children

Seth L. Goldstein, J.D., has started a non-profit forensic service called The Child Abuse Forensic Institute. The purpose of this organization is to assist parents or children if they feel they are in need of expert advice or are engaged in civil litigation involving child abuse allegations. For more information contact the Institute at 2827 Concord Boulevard, Concord, CA 94519. Telephone: (510) 682-4040.

APPENDIX B

What To Do, Step-By-Step, If Your Child Is Lost or Missing

What To Do If Your Child Is Lost

Turn around for a minute and your child will have crawled between the clothes racks or wandered to look at toys in a department store. Luckily, the child is normally lost for just for a few seconds or minutes. Still, in that few minutes the fear you experience is immeasurable.

You can't keep your eye on your children every second (although until children reach an age where they can understand that they must not walk or run away from you, parents have to make every effort not to let them out of their sight). You must plan ahead to make sure you find your child fast if he or she is ever lost at a ball field, an amusement park, the mall, or wherever. Children won't know what to do when they're lost unless you tell them ahead of time. It is reassuring to know that you and your children have a "lost and found" plan if you are ever separated. Then both of you will take the necessary steps and avoid the immobilization that panic can bring about.

If your child is ever lost, you should not assume that he will turn up in just a few minutes. One story from *America's Most Wanted* illustrates this rule: a three-year-old child disappeared from her parents' side in a Walmart store. Once the parents realized that their daughter was lost, the parents told the manager. He immediately implemented the store's new "Code Adam" program for lost children. Employees hurried to all the exits to lock the doors. Soon they found a middle age man trying to get out one of the back doors

167

of the store with the child. The child turned to the store clerk and said, "Can you take me to my mommy please?"

Here are five step-by-step guidelines, recommended by The SAFE-T-CHILD Program, that parents should follow if their child is ever lost:

1. Act now – time is crucial. It is important to stay as calm as possible so that you can think and communicate thoroughly.

2. Enlist help. Call a security guard, policeman, store manager, or whomever you can get to help you look for your child. If your child is lost you want as many people looking as possible. If you are in a place with a public-address speaker system, use it to call for your child.

3. Give authorities an accurate description of your child. An immediate response I.D. card is invaluable in this situation. An incomplete description of your child will slow down the search – imagine how many three-foot high, brown-haired boys dressed in jeans there are in a mall on a Saturday afternoon. In the average mall, 10,000 people could pass through on a weekend day. At the very least, you should have a clear, up-to-date photograph of your child in your wallet.

4. Check every logical location, then fan out. If you have already taught your child to stay in the area where you were separated, then you can concentrate your search there. Or better yet, if you and your child have agreed on a meeting spot if you are ever separated, be sure you or someone stays in that spot to meet your child if they show up. If the child is lost at home or in your neighborhood, make sure to check the house from top to bottom. One telling example of this guideline occurred one summer afternoon when a mother couldn't find her six-year-old daughter. She immediately enlisted other parents' and children's help, and they began searching all over the neighborhood. After

almost two hours of frantic searching, her older sister found her sleeping under her mother's bed. After searching your own home, check with all of your child's friends and look in or call the places he or she normally spends time.

5. Plan ahead to help prevent trouble in public places. Many parents have a variety of ways they use to help ensure their children stay close to them and to help find their children quickly if they are ever lost. Here are a few:

• Stay on your toes. Children are incredibly fast and naturally curious.

• Dress your children in distinctive clothing so that they will stand out in a crowd. Some parents have even done something creative such as tie colorful helium balloons to their children's wrist.

• At a crowded beach, one frantic mother looked for her three-year-old child by kneeling to the ground and looking through all of the long adult legs. She found him right away.

• At a stadium or auditorium, write the child's section and seat number on the back of their hands.

• Thoroughly discuss with your child what to do if they are lost and explain to them what you will do to find them. In public places agree to a meeting spot if you are separated.

• When you find your child, remember that this is not the time to reprimand them for getting lost. Instead, let them know you are glad to see them and praise them for being smart or brave.

What To Do If Your Child is Missing

The most important point to remember if your child is ever missing is to take action immediately, even if you think he may have left voluntarily. Runaways become victims of street criminals and organized crime more often than most people realize. In the eyes of the law, minors are not held responsible for their decisions so they certainly should not be expected to make crucial decisions that their very lives may depend on. We hope the following points will also help to speed-up your reunion:

1. File a missing persons report with your local police or sheriff. There is no rule that the police must wait 24 hours before they consider your child missing. Also (in the U.S.A.), if a child is over 18 years old you can file a report with the Salvation Army's Department of Missing Persons. Be truthful in reporting family conflicts and/or relationships or other unpleasant circumstances. Authorities are critically handicapped if they do not have all the facts and circumstances leading up to your child's disappearance. Which is more important – your pride or your child's life?

2. Ask your local police to register data with the National Crime Information Center (NCIC) and your State Bureau of Investigation. Follow up with a call to your nearest FBI office to verify entry in the NCIC computer in Washington, DC. They will enter it for you if the police have not. In Canada make sure the provincial police and RCMP (the Canadian Missing Persons division) have the information. The National Center for Missing and Exploited Children functions in Canada and the U.S.A.: to file information call 1-800-843-5678. Child Find of America is also in both Canada and the U.S.A.: for Child Find/U.S.A. call 1-800-426-5678; in Canada call 1-800-387-7962. You can reach the Missing Children Society of Canada at 1-800-661-6160. You may also contact

Operation Lookout/The National Center for Missing Youth at (800) 782-7335.

3. Stay in close touch with your jurisdictional authorities. Insist that they follow up on all leads, to your full satisfaction. Keep a file with all of the authorities you have dealt with including each officer's name and badge number, your case numbers, and records of all information concerning the investigation.

4. When searching for your child, don't leave a stone unturned. One thing you can do is to retrace the last known steps your child took. Do it at the same time of day as the disappearance, because people who regularly travel that route may be valuable witnesses. Don't assume that police are giving highest priority to the search for your child. Ongoing crimes may take precedence. But keep yourself in their awareness by calling regularly. Also insist that authorities accept all outside offers of help.

5. If your child does not return within 24 hours and there is no indication that the child ran away, ask your jurisdictional police agency (in the U.S.A.) to request an FBI investigation (NOTE: In some cases you do not have to wait 24 hours to request the FBI). The Federal Kidnapping Statute states that when a kidnapping victim is not released within 24 hours, it can be presumed he has been taken across a state line. (This pertains to parental kidnapping as well.) The FBI is authorized by the Parental Kidnapping Prevention Act of 1980 to search for abducted children taken across state lines. Similar procedures should be followed in Canada with the RCMP.

6. Keep a pencil and paper by the telephone to record any information received. Even better, have a tape recorder handy to record messages and voices. If you think your child might try to reach you or someone you know by phone, keep phones manned 24 hours a day. If you are concerned that your child doesn't know your area code, you

may want to call your telephone number at all existing area codes. Explain your situation to people at these numbers and ask for their help if your child calls.

7. Always keep your old phone number if you ever have a missing child. You can generally make special arrangements with the phone company to keep your old number active if you move and you have lost a child. If this service is available in your area, tell your child that you will always keep that number if you are ever separated.

8. Offer a reward and distribute posters. Note: In some cases posters are more dangerous than helpful, because it may cause an abductor to leave the area due to the fear of being apprehended. If it is decided that it would be beneficial to use posters in your case, make sure to use a current photo. Also include the circumstances of the disappearance and the date and the place the child was last seen. Post these flyers everywhere that seems worthwhile. Publicizing your child's photo may help someone recognize him and contact the authorities. If the child did run away and happens to see the story or the posters (which reflect your concern for your child), he may be encouraged to call home or try to get back to you.

9. Call the local runaway hotline (U.S.A.) as well as the National Switchboard at 1-800-621-4000. You can leave a message for your child and find out if your child left you one. Let your child know that you are willing to listen.

10. Check for unidentifiable children at hospitals and morgues.

11. If you hire a private detective, choose carefully. You may be approached by several private detectives. Be sure to check references and the Better Business Bureau.

12. If your child has runaway and is over 18 years old:
   • Check your credit cards to see if there are purchases

that are not yours. This information could help locate your child or the abductor.

• If a car is involved, check with your state's motor vehicle registration department.

• If your child is working and has a Social Security Number, the Social Security Department will send a letter from you to your missing child's last known address. You must give proof that your child is missing along with specific information required for the records search.

• Check on passports at your State Department (or with the provincial government in Canada).

• Check with the local recruiting offices and the national headquarters of each branch of the service to see if your child has joined the armed services.

This Appendix was written, in part, from material published by the National Center for Missing and Exploited Children.

APPENDIX C

Child Security
Products and Services

To help keep your children safe, you may want to consider purchasing some of the many child security products and services in the marketplace. This section will give you an overview of most of the child security products that are available, and provide you with the relative advantages and limitations of each one. (We have omitted the products and services that are new and require further development and testing.)

It is important to evaluate the child safety products and services before you purchase them so that you can avoid two key problems: 1. developing a feeling of security because you have purchased a safety product or service, when, in fact, the product or service may not be truly as effective as is claimed (parents must always keep in mind that no product or service replaces solid personal safety education); and 2. purchasing a child safety product or service from a non-reputable company. There are several companies offering parents child security products; most are reputable, but unfortunately there are a handful of companies who are little more than opportunists seeking to capitalize on parents' fears. Many of these companies have either failed, have poor or misrepresented products, or limited, incomplete, or wrong information. For the most effective products and for the greatest security of your privacy, you should only deal with reputable child security companies or organizations.

Before purchasing child security products or services, you should ask yourself: Are these tools really helpful? The following information will give you a frame of reference for evaluation. And because rarely is one product or service enough to ensure your child's security, the information in this section will also help you plan a complete child security system for your children.

I.D. Products and Services

Child identification. What exactly does that mean? In today's world it means more than just giving authorities a sketchy description of your child. "He's three-and-a-half feet tall, blond hair, and blue jeans . . ." That type of information means nothing in today's crowded amusement parks, malls, and ball parks. As mentioned earlier, 10,000 people may pass through a typical mall on a Saturday afternoon. Compounding the confusing issue of child identification is the wide variety of child I.D. products on the market (the selection is growing as several companies move to enter the marketplace). How is a parent supposed to know whether the I.D. products being advertised in Sunday's paper are products that they really need or just another product that will give them a sense of security, but, in reality, do nothing to help protect their child?

While identification products and services are an important part of a complete family safety program remember this one important fact: child I.D. products are for when a problem occurs. Just like insurance, you hope you never actually have to use it, but you should be prepared. Here are the child I.D. products you need to know about:

Child Identification (I.D.) Cards

A child I.D. card is the most convenient and effective form of child identification, because parents and guardians carry the I.D. cards in their purses and wallets just like a driver's license. There is no better way for parents to instantly provide identification of their lost or missing child to authorities. For maximum benefit, these child I.D. cards must be properly prepared and contain the exact information that is required by authorities to find a lost or missing child. (See the chapter called, "Carry Proper I.D. - It's Critical" for a listing of the key information necessary on a child I.D. card.) Some I.D. cards also carry medical emergency information, which can be valuable if your child has special medical requirements. Also, I.D. cards should be laminated whenever possible, so that they do not become smudged, bent, or tattered. Unfortunately, many I.D. cards are incomplete or poorly made. To be truly effective, every parent and guardian should carry I.D. cards for each of their children. You should also keep an extra card handy for babysitters, relatives, or friends to carry when they are watching your child. It's also valuable for children to carry I.D. cards on them. If they are injured or lost, the identifying information can help medical and law enforcement personnel assist them and contact you. Keep in mind that the cards should be concealed so that no one can gain access to the information. Your children can keep the cards in their backpacks, wallets, fanny packs, or purses.

Front of SAFE•T•CHILD Immediate Response I.D.™ Card

177

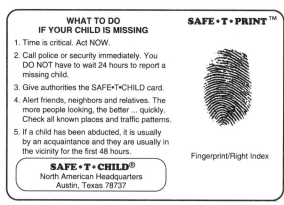

**WHAT TO DO
IF YOUR CHILD IS MISSING**

SAFE•T•PRINT ™

1. Time is critical. Act NOW.
2. Call police or security immediately. You DO NOT have to wait 24 hours to report a missing child.
3. Give authorities the SAFE•T•CHILD card.
4. Alert friends, neighbors and relatives. The more people looking, the better ... quickly. Check all known places and traffic patterns.
5. If a child has been abducted, it is usually by an acquaintance and they are usually in the vicinity for the first 48 hours.

Fingerprint/Right Index

SAFE•T•CHILD®
North American Headquarters
Austin, Texas 78737

Rear of SAFE•T•CHILD Immediate Response I.D.™ Card

Child I.D. Cards have been used successfully many times in real-life situations. These cards can be obtained from child identification and security companies, through mall or business promotions, occasionally from police, and in do-it-yourself kits. Home-made cards are generally of a lower quality, but they still offer a valuable and convenient form of immediate response identification, especially if no I.D. card service is available in your area. For information on how to obtain I.D. cards through The SAFE-T-CHILD Program in or near your community, or to order the I.D. Card Kits, which allow you to make the cards at home, please refer to the ordering information in the back of this book.

Note: For families' privacy and security, we do not recommend that any personal information, such as photographs, fingerprints, and videos, be kept by anyone but the child's parents or guardians. That is why, in the United States and Canada, neither SAFE-T-CHILD nor its Directors retain any of this confidential information. (Other countries may require private registration services.)

DNA I.D.

DNA I.D. is, without question, the future of identification. For one thing, DNA I.D. (also known as "genetic fingerprinting") is the only virtually positive and permanent identification method. For example, photographs fade and must be updated, and fingerprints can smear or be difficult to acquire (getting a proper child's fingerprint can be very difficult), but each person's DNA does not change for his entire life. DNA (deoxyribonucleic acid) molecules are that part of the human physiology which carries the genetic "blueprint" that makes each person unique. Each person's "genetic" makeup is exclusive and never changes for their entire life. As such, "DNA fingerprinting" can provide reliable identification even when it may be impossible to recover a fingerprint. Further, DNA I.D. is generally admissible in court, and can be invaluable in reuniting parents with their children in the case of parental abductions, kidnappings, accidents, and natural disasters.

DNA identification is now available to families in an easy-to-use, at-home kit. With the "do-it-yourself" DNA I.D.™ Kit, it takes parents only minutes to capture, preserve, and store-at-home their child's genetic "fingerprints." Thousands of parents are already keeping their children's "genes" at home. The DNA I.D. Kit provides a way of properly taking, recording, and storing genetic samples in a patented, tamper-proof system. It is a way of properly <u>storing</u> genetic samples, not the actual test. If the DNA sample is ever needed to make a genetic match the process is usually initiated by law enforcement or some other agency. (Beware of suggestions to "make your own DNA I.D." While storing DNA samples at home can be simple with a specially made medical product, it can be completely ineffective without the right procedures.) The DNA I.D. Kit can also be a part of your at-home fact file. By combining an up-to-date child I.D. card and the DNA I.D. Kit, parents can have a valuable child identification system.

DNA is so important to the future of identification that it is already being used by the FBI and the U.S. services. In fact, DNA I.D. is the preferred method of identification for law enforcement, as seen in more and more court cases recently. "DNA Analysis . . . is considered the most important advance in forensics since fingerprinting. Its use in U.S. courts has skyrocketed from 14 cases by the end of 1987 to 12,000 by mid-1993," according to an article in the *Austin-American Statesman* in June 1994. The FBI is implementing a national DNA database, called CODIS, to track people by their DNA. The U.S. Army started a genetic depository in 1992 that will eventually include the DNA of every American in uniform. The U.S. Army's goal is to have no more "unknown soldiers." DNA is also already being used to identify missing children. For example, in December, 1993, a two-year old was returned to his parents two years after being kidnapped – only after police established scientifically who the child was by using "genetic fingerprinting." To order the DNA I.D.™ Kit, refer to information at the back of the book.

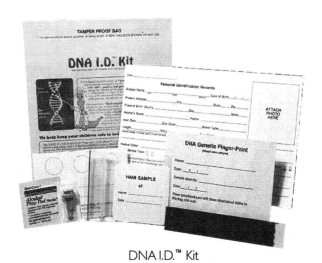

DNA I.D.™ Kit

Fingerprints

Fingerprinting children is one of the most popular child identification methods by organizations, especially at community events and malls. Many parents are lead to believe that a set of fingerprints will keep their child safe. However, fingerprints of children do nothing to prevent abduction, and they are not a replacement for Immediate Response I.D. cards. They are generally only valuable if a child is missing long-term. What's more, fingerprints of children are extremely difficult to get even by professionals, such as police. In fact, authorities find that up to 75 percent of the fingerprints taken of children may be of little value. The reason is that the lines on a child's fingers are very fine. That's why foot and palm prints are often taken of very young children. It therefore takes a special touch to ensure that the ink is not too heavy or too light, that the correct angle on the finger is used, and that at least 10 of the ridges and valleys of the pattern are clear. For this reason, parents should be sure that fingerprints are taken by people trained to take fingerprints of children and who do so regularly. Whenever possible, they should avoid trying to do it themselves at home. However, they are better than nothing until you can get them done by professionals. Fingerprints of your child, either one good one or a whole set, should be kept in an at-home fact file. If you only have one clear print, it should be the index finger of the right or left hand (depending on whether the child is right or left handed), because that is the finger your child is most likely to touch with and leave a readable print behind.

Home I.D. Record File

Another important child identification method is a child I.D. home record stored in a safe place. An at-home I.D. record of your child provides thorough identification of a lost child. Again, however, it does not replace proper

I.D. that you carry on your person. The advantage of a home record file is that it can contain more information than a wallet I.D. card, and is useful primarily for more long-term missing children.

Parents should assemble an at-home identification packet for each of their children. Include in this packet:

• Recent photographs of your child (the photographs need to be straight on to be useful for identification, reproduction, and photo-aging techniques), including a clear, color head and shoulders shot that accurately depicts what your child looks like;

• An accurate physical description of your child including height and weight, hair and eye colors, scars and birthmarks, glasses, braces, earrings;

• Up-to-date medical and dental records;

• Fingerprints (see above);

• A videotape of your child; and

• Any information that could help identify or locate your child, for example the names, addresses and numbers of friends, common play areas, mannerisms, and habits.

Parents should store this information in a safe place in their home. Also, they should consider carrying a copy of this information with them if they are on an extended vacation. Since children grow and change quickly, parents should update this information at least once every year. While some sources recommend four times a year for preschoolers, that is not practical for most busy families. Do it as often as you can manage, but for sure once a year. If you have a properly organized home record file, it will be much easier to update.

Photographs

There are very specific requirements for a photograph

that will be useful to find a child. As mentioned above, a good photo means a clear, color head and shoulders shot that accurately depicts what your child looks like. It must be a front view and be very sharp. Because children grow and change quickly, photos must be updated regularly.

Video tapes

Video footage of your child provides authorities an opportunity to see the child from a variety of angles. Be sure to keep the videos safely at home in a fact file. You do not have to pay a lot of money for any "special" kinds of video footage, just use your video camera or borrow a friend's. From time to time, some video operations and businesses offer special child video promotions in some communities.

Child I.D. Jewelry

The value of I.D. jewelry – bracelets, necklaces and shoe tags – is fundamentally the same as the child carrying their own I.D. card. If your child is injured or can't communicate for whatever reason, the I.D. can help law enforcement and medical personnel contact you. But so that you don't advertise your child's name, the information on the bracelet and shoe tags should be on the inside only. Also, the engraving on necklaces should be fine enough that no one can read it unless they are very close and hold the tag correctly in the light. Shoe tags are better than iron-

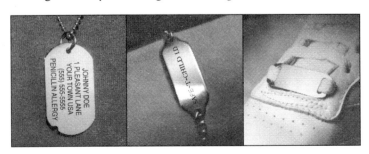

on labels because children usually have fewer shoes than they do pants and shirts. Also, the tags can be transferred to new shoes as your child grows. The drawback, of course, is that if you are going to use them, they should be on all the child's shoes. The value of a bracelet or necklace is that you only need one and it is always on your child. I.D. jewelry can often be purchased at mall "kiosks," jewelry stores, and flea markets. Our "I.D. Pals" are offered through mail order at the back of this book.

Iron-On I.D. Labels

Iron-on I.D. labels are generally sold in two forms. One type has your child's name, address, and telephone number. The other type is generally issued as part of a "child registration" service. The only information that appears on the label is your child's name and a central contact number, which is often an 800 number. If you register with such a service, make sure you are careful about who is keeping personal information on your child.

There are two fundamental problems with iron-on labels. The first problem is just one of practicality. It is difficult for parents to keep current labels in all the articles of clothing of a growing child. Not only do children grow rapidly, they lose things and they destroy things. As a result, for many busy parents it is almost impossible to stay current with labels. The second problem is that law enforcement, medics, or other people who may be assisting your child in the case of an emergency may not even notice the labels on your child's clothing. I.D. jewelry, on the other hand, generally is easy to spot.

Photo-aging techniques

Increasingly, photo-aging techniques have had a measure of success. In this process, a photo of a child is "age progressed" to try and determine what a child, who was last seen years ago, may look like today. However, parents must keep in mind that this technique is only educated guess-work. It can not identify a lost child with 100% accuracy. Up until recently, the process of age progressed photos was tedious and time consuming, often taking up to 36 hours by a professional police artist or medical illustrator. Recently, computerized age progression technology has been developed. To age progress a child's photo, the artists enhance the facial features based on the child's parents' and siblings' features. To be effective, parents must be involved in the process because they can provide key descriptions of family members. While computerized age progression is faster, it is still a painstaking process, where specially trained artists must work on one section of the child's face at a time. While not necessarily an accurate depiction of the child at his or her current age, this process can give the families some measure of hope in rekindling public interest and generating new leads.

Personal Alarms and Monitoring Devices

Personal alarms emit a piercing shriek or siren when the child pulls a pin or activates it by some other method. Some are even two-way with the adult and child each wearing units. The purpose of monitoring devices is to allow adults to pinpoint a child's location within a certain range. But so far the effectiveness of alarms and monitors is still being studied. As we previously mentioned, no product should be purchased as a replacement for child security education. "No neighborhood watch or electronic device can replace solid safety rules and emergency strategies for children," stated an article in the *Austin American-Statesman* on January 29, 1994. If parents feel strongly about using alarms and monitors, they must remember one important thing: they are not fail-safe so you cannot depend solely on them. Among the problems: your child may forget it when he leaves the house, the batteries may fail, it may get damaged in play, and it may not perform as promised. While they may be great attention-getters, the other side of the coin is that people don't necessarily respond to alarms because they have become desensitized to this type of noise. Better than alarms or monitors is a child who knows how to properly scream, "This is not my mom!" or other appropriate phrases. Their voice will never be left at home and will not run out of battery power. If you purchase an alarm or monitor, do so as a <u>complement</u> to a family safety program, which includes well-rounded education. Make sure to purchase the devices from reputable companies.

Martial Arts

Gaining skill in a martial art can be a valuable personal safety tool, but not for the reasons most people think. Most experts agree that martial arts classes will not help a child physically defend himself against an adult attacker. According to Officer Dan "The Hulk" Razzano: "I don't care what kind of belt they have. Black belt. Green belt. A six-year-old is not going to beat an older person out there in a street brawl when the person wants to get the child." (HBO's "How to Raise a Street Smart Kid," video). Often children see images on TV or at the movies of children "beating up" adults, and they think they can do it, too. "Three Ninjas" is a great example. It's a fun family movie – but no reality whatsoever. In fact, if a child tries to fight back with an adult, he may only further enrage the person.

However, according to those involved in martial arts, the skills learned do have important benefits. At the very least, your child can gain much needed confidence, self-esteem, and important life skills. The right kind of martial arts training helps educate the mind and the body. That can be truly powerful safety training. According to Sensei

David Ham, member of the Aikikai Foundation (Japan), "When a child stops fighting and starts taking positive action to remain safe is when self-defense really works. And taking positive action is only possible with proper safety training." Furthermore, when children gain confidence through self-defense they realize that they don't generally need to fight to stay safe. Instead, they learn to steer clear of problems in the first place. The bottom line: the best way for a child to defend himself against an attacker is to use his common sense and personal safety skills.

Educational Products

As you know, we think these are the most important products of all. However, just because an educational product is on the market does not mean that it is a good product; or even if it is valuable, that does not mean it is a complete child security system. You must use discrimination, and apply the principles you have learned in this book. If you do purchase a safety educational product or enroll your child in a safety education program, you should review, test, and challenge what your child has learned so you can help customize it to the unique circumstances of your child and your family situation.

There is a variety of safety education products, including music, books, computer games, and videos, that are generally available from your local library, book stores, music stores, video stores, or direct from private organizations. Programs offered in communities or through schools should also be considered. One of the most notable is *Kids and Company: Together for Safety,* a program of the National Center for Missing and Exploited Children through its educational division, the Adam Walsh Children's Fund. (You can reach NCMEC at (703) 235-3900.) This school-based education program is organized into six sections with videos and workbooks designed for each section. The lessons stress "role-playing" and testing.

The SAFE-T-CHILD Program, which includes seminars, books, music, literature, and identification products and services, is also available to schools, daycares, churches, civic organizations, and business sponsors. For more information about the SAFE-T-CHILD Program, see the information at the back of this book.

Missing Children Organizations

There are many fine, non-profit organizations that are doing valuable work in the area of child safety education. Many offer valuable services and information to the public. They operate on national, regional, and/or local levels. Each one has their own particular focus. They are too numerous to mention here, but if you ask around in your community, you should be able to locate one that is active in your area. You may also contact the National Center for Missing and Exploited Children at (703) 235-3900 and they will refer you to organizations operating in your area.

APPENDIX D

Yello Dino Music

Music: The Charming Way to Safer Children

A song is more than just words and a melody. It is a singer, a mood, a setting, a story, and characters. With educational songs – particularly safety education – the creators of music have a further responsibility because they have to impart valuable educational concepts into enjoyable songs that children will want to hear again and again. It's much harder than it sounds!

What's more, we wanted to create safety education songs that the difficult-to-reach 10-to-12-year-olds would like as much as the four-to-nine-year-olds. Today's pre-teens are just too sophisticated for what they perceive as "baby" songs, and too often educational music talks down to children. We know that to make music truly effective, kids have to like it. So our goal was to create *great* songs that just happened to have a message. In fact, we wanted to weave safety education into music that is so enjoyable children don't even realize how strong of an effect the songs have on them. The best educational songs should be so memorable that children can remember the words at the (often stressful) moment that they need the knowledge.

To accomplish this task, we called on the talents of some of the music industry's best and brightest. Most notably among these music professionals is our songwriter and producer, David Ham. David has won over a thousand broadcast awards, including nine Clio nominations for radio (advertising's highest award), three international

Broadcast Awards, and six Best of Canada Awards in his long and respected music career. Many of the music and educational professionals involved in this first album, *Can't Fool Me!*, were as inspired as we were to be a part of this important project of getting valuable safety information to children. To ensure that this music was as valuable as it could be, every word, every lyric, every singer, and the musical style of every song was chosen specifically to accomplish a particular safety objective.

The main character of our safety education program for children is Yello Dino (pronounced "dye-no"). He is the ultimate big brother to every child. He is big, strong, and, unless you mess with his kids, he is friendly to everyone. Kids say he's "cool" – the utmost praise from four-to-12-year-olds. Most importantly, he knows all of the important safety rules and cares most about sharing them with children. You and your children will be seeing a lot of Yello Dino in our upcoming safety education albums and safety education materials.

It is only through music that the safety rules can evoke the deep, strong, emotional and psychological lessons for children. Here are the wonderful lyrics to *Can't Fool Me!*, and a little bit about how and why we created each song.

Yello Dino's "CAN'T FOOL ME!" Volume 1
Available on Cassette or CD

The Yello Dino Yell

Like an energetic pep rally, Yello Dino himself leads off the *Can't Fool Me!* safety music concert to a "foot-stomping" start by teaching boys and girls how to yell for help properly. With his "cool," soulful "Blues Brothers" personality he cuts right through children's lack of understanding about what makes a "from-the-gut" yell that will truly attract attention. Yello Dino's playful dialogue also breaks down children's natural embarrassment about yelling to attract attention to themselves in public places. And Yello Dino also teaches children important phrases to yell if they are ever in trouble, such as "This is not my dad!" What kid won't love being let in on the ancient "Paleozoic secret" of yelling?

Intro Announcer: Ladies and Gentlemen ...What all y'all have been waitin' for ... would you welcome ... quiet down now ... quiet down ... would you please welcome ... that Purveyor of Protection, that paleontolic personality, that barry totin', foot-stompin', tail-thumpin', safety maven o' soul ... brothers and sisters... give it up for Yello Dino!

YD: (laugh) YEAH!

[Audience Goes Nuts]

YD: Let me hear you say YEAH!

Crowd: Yeah

YD: Let me hear you say YEAH!

Crowd: Yeah

YD: Let me hear you say YEAH!

Crowd: Yeah

YD: YEAH!

Crowd: Yeah

YD: YEAH!

Crowd: Yeah

YD: YEAH! Oh, oh, no, hold the band...

[Band Stops Playing]

YD: Now you gonna have ta do better than that on the yell. Ol' Yello Dino just can't get the band motivated with that performance. Let's try the girls. I'll say "Yeah," you say "Yeah" back. OK? Ready? *YEAH!*

Girls: Yeah!

YD: Now the boys, *YEAH!*

Boys: Yeah!

YD: Now together, *YEEAAAH!*

Both: Yeeaah!

YD: That's pretty good. But I just don't think that's gonna get the band started. That right guys?

[Squeak From Band]

YD: See what I mean? I tell you what. I'll share with you an ancient dino secret handed down to me from my family over one million years ago. It's the secret of the *Yello Dino Yell!* (laugh) O.K. girls, you first. Take your breath way down, down, ... 2" past the belly button. Take a big breath and let it out. Ready? *YEAAAAAH!*

Girls: *YEEAAH!!*

YD: Wow! Now boys! *YEAAAAAH!*

Boys: *YEEAAH!!*

YD: Yeah! Now you got to help me y'all. You got to get down, you got to give me some help. And as you know, we all need help sometimes. So when you need help ... you got to have it. You got to say "Help, this is not my DAD!" Go!

Both: Help! This is not my DAD!

YD: Yeah! And you say, "Help! This is not my MOM!"

Both: Help! This is not my MOM!

YD: Yes! "Help! This is not my BROTHER!"

Both: Help! This is not my BROTHER!

YD: Yes! You have done it. You have the ancient secret! You have the power! The Power of the Yello Dino Yell! YEEEAAAAH!

MUSIC: Dino Stomp

Announcer: Ladies and Gentlemen. Give it up for that paleontolic personality, that safety maven of soul – Yello Dino!

YD: Hope you enjoy the Show ... and remember ... *SAFETY RULES!*

Tricky People

We thought that a cool, classic rock and roll tune was the best way to help children understand a difficult topic – the tricks adults use to lure children. This approach is a far cry from the "big, dark stranger on a corner" concept of "bad" adults that children often conjure up when left to their own imaginations. This song had two main objectives: to help children recognize the tricks used by "tricky" people and to instruct them on what to do if they are ever approached by a tricky person. The engaging female singer instructs kids about tricky people using four typical scenarios ("lures") in a completely non-fearful way. She also helps make the safety rules for dealing with "tricky" people's lures practical and down-to-earth.

Verse 1
What if you see a guy in town
Who wants his puppy found
What do you do when he asks
    for help
And no one is around

Take three steps back
Take three steps back
That's how you can begin
Take three steps back
Take three steps back
Then run like the wind

Chorus 1
Tricky people
    Tricky, tricky people
They look like you and me
Tricky people
    Tricky, tricky people
Are bent where you can't see

Verse 2
What if a person tells you that
Your family's hurt and down
What do you do when they say come
And no one can be found

"What's my code?"
"Hey, what's my code?"
That's how you can begin
If they don't know
Take three steps back
Then run like the wind

Chorus 2
Tricky people
    Tricky, tricky people
Have pain down in their heart

They're tricky people
They can't fool me
'Cause I'm too smart

Verse 3
What if a guy shows you a badge
And he says he's a cop
Now, what do you do?
    How do you check?
Before you go - you stop!

You call 9-1-1
Or you call "O"
That's how you begin
And if they say "NO!"
Take three steps back,
And then run like the wind

[Repeat Chorus 1]

Verse 4
What if a guy gives you some cash
If you'll go with him now
What if the little voice inside of you
Says "No sir," "No way," No how!"

Take three steps back
Take three steps back
That's how you begin
Take three steps back
    Three steps back
Then run like the wind

[Repeat Chorus 2]

195

Help Me Operator

What better way to ensure that children remember their telephone numbers, including their often forgotten or difficult-to-remember area code, than to set them to music? And while we're at it, why not teach them how to dial "0" and "911" for emergencies and tell them what to say when they get the operator on the line? This may at first glance seem like a song only for young children, but many older children do not know their area codes because they never have to use them. Similarly, most children have never had to call an operator for an emergency, so they are unsure of exactly what to do. The pace of this "bluesy shuffle" not only gives kids the correct tempo for memorization, it will also help calm them down when they sing it to themselves if they are ever in an emergency situation.

If you have an emergency
Pick up the phone and dial "O"
(tone)

Verse 1
Help me Operator
Tell me what I should do
I need some help
And I've got to get through
I just dialed "O"
And I'm talkin' to you
And here's another little thing
That you can do

Chorus 1
Dial 9-1-1
Dial 9-1-1
Say your name and problem
Say your address too

Dial 9-1-1
Dial 9-1-1
Say your name and problem
And your address too

Verse 2
Can you say
Your telephone number
My friend
Area Code first

And then you begin
First you dial ONE
First dial ONE
Now we're going to practice
"Ready and ONE" (tone)

[Chorus 2 - Sing-along]

Verse 3
Let me hear
Your telephone number again
Area Code first
And then you begin
First you dial ONE
First dial ONE
Now let's sing it
"Ready and ONE" (tone)

[Chorus 2 - Sing-along]

Verse 4
It really is so simple
It's actually fun
"O" for Operator
Or dial 9-1-1
Say your name and problem
Say your address too
Sing your phone number
I'm so proud of you

[Chorus 2 - Sing-along]

We Trust Our Feelings

This charming ballad reawakens children's natural instincts and feelings "way down inside." Unfortunately, even when we are very young we start to believe that our natural instincts may not be valid or can't be trusted. The sweet, motherly female singer in this song not only lets children know that their inner feelings really exist and that those feelings deserve respect, she explains to them that these feelings have a tremendous amount of power behind them that can actually help keep them safe. You can almost see her hugging each child as she sings, "When you trust your inner feelings you'll have an ocean on your side."

Verse 1
There's a light up in the sky
It's no bigger than your eye
And it shines upon the earth
It's there at each and every birth

You see it lives way down inside
And it's there for all your life
You know it's really very smart
It's the light of your heart

Chorus 1
And this sweet light acts like an ocean
Warm, whirling, moving deep inside
And this light is our true feelings
We trust our feelings all the time

Verse 2
So when your light says something's
    wrong
You should act - not wait too long

When you're feeling all alone
You have the power to be strong

You touch the light down in your heart
It's so easy - just a thought
It's the same around the world
For every guy and every girl

Chorus 1
And this sweet light acts like an ocean
Warm, whirling, moving deep inside
And this light is our true feelings
We trust our feelings all the time

Chorus 2
Can you feel your own heart light?
Like the ocean moving deep inside
When you trust your inner feelings
You'll have an ocean on your side
You'll have an ocean on your side

My Body's Mine

There are songs that are just meant to be danced to, songs that even if you wanted to you couldn't stop your body from moving to the beat. So it's appropriate that a song that teaches children that they have rights regarding their bodies should be a song that you just *have* to move your body to. This Caribbean dance tune teaches children in a fun way that they can choose the level of physical affection that is comfortable to them. It also approaches the sometimes difficult-to-talk-about-topic of "private parts" in a fun, playful manner – "what my bathing suit covers is private and mine, and that's a safety rule." Also, this song's lyrics are the kind that you just can't get out of your head, especially five little words that will help children keep themselves safer: "My body's mine, mine, mine!"

Chorus 1
My body's mine
    Mine, mine
My body's mine
    Mine, mine
I can take it to school
I can keep my cool
'Cause you know my body's mine

My body's mine
    Mine, mine
My body's mine
    Mine, mine
I am no fool
I play by the rules
'Cause I know my body's mine

Verse 1
Just the other day
A lady came up to me
She said "This is the cutest little guy
That I have ever seen"
And then she hugged
So tight my air was gone
So I said "NO! That hurts me so"
And sang my body song

[Repeat Chorus]

Verse 2
Well wouldn't you know
I saw this stranger in the mall
He looked real nice
But I thought twice
And you know that I said "NO!"
And then I moved
At least three steps back
In my heart was a bell
So I ran to tell
And I sang my song like that

[Repeat Chorus]

Verse 3
Well we all know
When we go to the pool
What my bathing suit covers
Is private and mine
And that's a safety rule
You don't touch me there
'Cause I will run and tell
It's against the law
And I'll tell what I saw
And sing my body song

[Repeat Chorus]

G.O.M.F.

There was only one way to give children the attitude they need to walk away from an adult who might try to strike up an inappropriate conversation, or "lay a rap," with them – a country and western boogie. Most children are polite to adults, but to follow the safety rule of not talking to people they do not know, children may have to "cut the dialogue" with an adult at some point in their life. This song gives them that right. The strong male singer in G.O.M.F. (Get Outta My Face) instructs them how to best do that – "you can do it kinda clumsy or you can do it with grace" – and he gives children the confidence, or "attitude," to accomplish what can be a difficult task for a child. This song also talks to kids in a way they can understand so that they can keep themselves safe – and, hey, if an adult ever attempts to cross your child's safety line your child can just "tell that big turkey, hey, get out of my face."

Verse 1
I'm the kinda kid
Who likes to go to town
I play a little ball
You can say I get around

But here's a little something
You just might want to know
In case

Chorus 1
If a stranger comes to you
And starts to lay a rap
Don't hang around
Don't fall for his trap

Take three steps back

It's a natural fact

You can do it kinda clumsy
You can do it with grace
But you tell that big turkey
"Hey, Get Outta My Face"

Verse 2
You see I'd rather be safe
Than always polite
Your mom or dad will tell you
That night after night

'Cause some apples taste great
Some apples have a worm

[Repeat Chorus 1]

Verse 3
So if after "Hello"
And you say "Hi" back
Cut the conversation
Take three steps back

'Cause even when it rains
You naturally run inside

Chorus 2
Ya got your eyes that can see
Ya got your ears that can hear
Ya got your heart that can feel
Ya got your feet that can get up
And run like the wind

"Hey Jack, Get Outta My Face"

You can do it kinda clumsy
You can do it with grace
But you tell that big turkey
"Hey, Get Outta My Face"

203

If Your Parents Get Lost

If a child gets lost in a mall or ball park he has the task of getting himself found. To do that, he needs to do the right thing quickly and do it with confidence. First of all, this song sets up a sweet twist for the child: it's his *parents* who are lost, not him, and he must find them. By instructing children through the use of two specific stories about how children find their parents, this song dispels the two worst things a child can do if he is lost – wander around and look scared. The clear, strong, "walk tall" voice of the female singer and the soothing voice of the male singer do more than just tell children what to do, they evoke the feeling of strength and confidence that a child needs to "be the boss," to find a security guard or a mom with kids, and to find their "lost parents." Moreover, the last verse of this song gives children a strong message of hope: if they are ever lost, they can follow the safety rules "and in no time at all" find their lost parents.

Rhythm Chorus
Where did you go?
Where did you go?
You were right here just a moment
ago!

Verse 1
I'm awalkin' through the mall
I'm awalkin' real tall
I'm findin' help right here
I'll betcha mom's real scared

Mom's probably just runnin' behind
She'll do better next time

I find the lady at the counter
And I speak real clear
"I need some HELP!"
I'm gonna stick around here

Mom's probably just runnin' behind
She'll do better next time

[Repeat Rhythm Chorus]

Verse 2
I'm in a ballpark
And it's gettin' kinda dark

I yell for Dad real loud
I might even draw a crowd

Dad's probably just runnin' behind
He'll do better next time

I can find a mom with kids
I'll be glad if I did
Ah! a security guard
That wasn't very hard

Dad's probably just runnin' behind
He'll do better next time

[Repeat Rhythm Chorus]

Verse 3
So if your parents get lost
It's your turn to be the boss
I'll be walkin' real tall
And in no time at all
They'll be laughin' and cryin'
They showed up in no time

They'll be laughin' and cryin'
They showed up in no time

205

Safely Held In Your Heart
(Luke's Song)

This is our theme song. It was inspired by real-life feelings and events. "Safety Held In Your Heart" evokes all of the feelings of love and safeness for which every person from birth to old-age longs. In this family love ballad, a man, woman, and child express their deep and tender feelings of love for each other. The emotions beautifully expressed in this song are the very feelings why every parent works so hard to keep their children safe and the reason why each child believes he or she is worth keeping safe. Love is the most important safety rule, because a child who feels loved is a child who knows they are valued. This is a ballad that every family can make its very own.

Verse 1
Mother, I couldn't tell you
I had no words to say
Love you gave me so freely
I can never repay

Chorus 1
Safely held in your heart
Safely rocked in your arms
Love continues to grow
Today, my child is born

Verse 2
Darling, I have to tell you
I think you're wonderfully strong
You're my sweet inspiration
Oh, how lucky we are

Chorus 2
Safely held in your heart
Safely rocked in your arms
Love continues to grow
Today, our child is born

Verse 3
Father, I can't tell you
I have no words to say
Love you give me so freely
I can never repay

Chorus 3
Safely held in your heart
Safely rocked in your arms
Love continues to grow
And today, I am born

Choral Rounds
Safely held in your heart
   Safely held in your heart
Safely rocked in your arms
   Safely rocked in your arms
Safely held in your heart
   Safely held in your heart
Love continues to grow
Today, our child is born

Bibliography

Books

Brodkin, Margaret and Coleman Advocates for Children & Youth. Every Kid Counts. San Francisco: Harper Collins, 1993.

Cooper, Paulette and and Paul Noble. Reward. New York: Pocket Books/Div. of Simon & Schuster Inc., 1994.

Dana, Trudy K. "Safety Away From Home." Safe and Sound, pgs. 165-169 & 180-201. New York: McGraw-Hill, 1988.

Children's Express. Voices From The Future. ed. Susan Goodwillie. New York: Crown Publishers, 1993.

Eyre, Linda and Richard. 3 Steps to a Strong Family. New York: Simon & Schuster, 1994.

Faber, Adele and and Elaine Mazlish. How To Talk So Kids Will Listen & Listen So Kids Will Talk. New York: Avon Books, 1980.

Fancher, Vivian Kramer. Safe Kids: A Complete Child-Safety Handbook & Resource Guide for Parents. New York: John Wiley & Sons, Inc., 1991.

Golant, Susan. "Part III. In The World." Fifty Ways to Keep Your Child Safe, Los Angeles: Lowell House, 1992.

Goldstein, Seth L. The Sexual Exploitation of Children. Boca Raton: CRC Press, 1987.

Greif, Geoffrey L. and and Rebecca L. Hegar. When Parents Kidnap: The Families Behind the Headlines. New York: The Free Press, 1993.

Hollingsworth, Jan. Unspeakable Acts. New York: Congdon & Weed, 1986.

Kraizer, Sherryll Kerns. The Safe Child Book. New York: Dell Publishing Co., 1985.

Kyte, Kathy S. Play It Safe: The Kids Guide to Personal Safety and Crime Prevention. New York: Alfred A. Knopf, Inc., 1983.

McNamara, Joseph D. Safe & Sane. New York: Perigee Books, 1984.

Rossi, Jani Hart. Protect Your Child From Sexual Abuse. Seattle: Parenting Press, 1984.

Siegler, Ava L. What Should I Tell The Kids?: A Parent's Guide to Real Problems in the Real World. New York: Penguin Books USA, 1993.

Strasburger, Victor M.D. Getting Your Kids to Say "No" in the '90's When You Said "Yes" in the 60's. New York: Fireside Simon & Schuster, 1993.

Van Der Zande, Irene. Kidpower: Guide for Parents and Teachers. Santa Cruz: Kidpower, 1991.

W. L. Marshall, D. R. Laws and, and H. E. Barbaree. Handbook of Sexual Assault. New York: Plenum Press, 1990.

Magazine Articles

"The Tragedy of America's Missing Children." U. S. News & World Report, October 24, 1983, pp. 63-64.

"Protecting Kids: A Matter of Growing Concern." Time, November 18, 1985, pp. 47.

"How Not to Have a Missing Child." Good Housekeeping, February 1986, pp. 230.

Bibliography

"Keeping Hope Alive." <u>Newsweek</u>, November 27, 1989, pp. 95-96.

"Zachary Scott Comes Home." <u>Missing Children Report</u>, 1993, pp. 6-8.

Adler, Jerry. "Kids Growing Up Scared." <u>Newsweek</u>, January 10, 1994, pp. 43-50.

Andrews, Lori B. "Terrified Generation?" <u>Parents</u>, December, 1986, pp. 139-232.

Bawden, Jim. "Better Safe Than Sorry." <u>Starweek</u>, March 21-28, 1992, pp. 4-5.

Brannen, Tammy. "A Mother Describes Four Months of Anguish Since Her Little Girl Vanished Almost Before Her Eyes." pp. 132-136.

Burden, Ordway P. "John Walsh and the Most Wanted." <u>Texas Police Journal</u>,1994, pp. 8-9.

Cerra, Frances. "Missing Children: New Facts About Fingerprinting, Videotaping, and the Milk Carton Search." <u>Ms.</u>, January, 1986, pp. 14-16.

Gleick, Elizabeth. "America's Child." <u>People</u>, December 20, 1993, pp. 84-90.

Hodges, Heidi and Bonnie White. "From Visitation to Abduction: A Family's Nightmare." <u>Missing Children Report</u>, 1993, pp. 9-11.

Hoyt, Carolyn. "Child Abductions: What a Mom Must Know." <u>McCall's</u>, March, 1994, pp. 60-67.

Kantrowitz, Barbara. "Stalking The Children." <u>Newsweek</u>, December 20, 1993, pp. 28-29.

Levine, Mark and and Deirdre Martin. "Have You Seen Me?: Aging the Images of Missing Children." <u>Law Enforcement Technology</u>, June, 1991, pp. 34-40.

McCarty, Frank. "The Electronic Trail of Robert Lewis Smith." <u>Missing Children Report</u>, 1993, pp. 12-13.

O'Connell, Diane and and Paula Mielke. "Careful, Not Fearful." <u>Sesame Street Parents' Guide</u>, May, 1991, pp. 12-15.

Oldham-O'Hara, Carol. "Could You Please Take Me Home Now?" <u>Missing Children Report</u>, 1993, pp. 14-16.

Raab, Jamie. "Every Mother's Fear." <u>Family Circle</u>, March 25, 1986, pp. 24-130.

Runner, Deborah Wilson. "Welcome home, Brian" <u>Ladies' Home Journal</u>, September 1993, pp. 22-29.

Smolowe, Jill. "A High-Tech Dragnet." <u>Time</u>, November 1, 1993, p. 43.

Stepp, Laura Sessions. "Missing Children: The Ultimate Nightmare." <u>Parents</u>, April, 1994, pp. 47-52.

Thad, Martin. "Who's Stealing Our Children." <u>Ebony</u>, February, 1986, pp. 139-144.

Thuman, Michiela. "Missing Children." <u>American Baby</u>, October, 1985, pp. 54-60.

Van Biema, David. "Robbing The Innocents." <u>Time</u>, December 27, 1993, pp. 31-32.

Walsh, John. "The Story Behind the Picture." <u>Guideposts</u>, September, 1984, pp. 2-6.

Wright, Rosalind. "Where Are Our Children?" <u>Ladies' Home Journal</u>, March, 1994, pp. 118-196.

Newspaper Articles

"Quick Action Credited in Abducted Girl's Return." <u>Austin-American Statesman</u>, July 5, 1994.

Barden, J. C. "Amid Rising Divorce, Parents Are Abducting Thousands of Children." <u>The New York Times</u>, May 6, 1990.

Caldwell, Jean. "Rebecca Knew She Was in Danger When She Saw the Truck." <u>The Boston Globe</u>, January 17, 1994, p. 13.

Dreyfous, Leslie. "Awareness, Education Help Fight Abductions." <u>Austin American-Statesman</u>, Saturday, January 29, 1994.

Elliot, David. "When Stealing Children Is Legal." <u>Austin American-Statesman</u>, May 14, 1994.

Granados, Christine. "Child Pornography Arrest Shocks Neighbors." <u>Austin American-Statesman</u>, 1994.

Murphy, Sean P. "Beware of Kidnapper, Police Say." <u>The Boston Globe</u>, February 17, 1994.

Robertson, Alonza. "Parents Warned To Be Prepared." <u>Las Vegas Review-Journal/Sun</u>, April 10, 1994.

Santoli, Al. "A Better Way To Protect Our Children." <u>Parade</u>, July 24, 1994, pp. 12-13.

Wright, Scott W. and and Miguel M. Salinas. "Eash Missing Person Case is Different, Police Say." <u>Austin American-Statesman</u>, July, 1994.

Television Programs

ABC. *20/20.* "The Lures of Death." 1984.

ABC. *20/20.* "Can They Be Caught." 1984.

ABC. *20/20.* "They're Murdering Our Children." 1984.

ABC. *20/20.* "The Best Kept Secret." 1984.

ABC. *20/20.* "Why The Silence." 1985.

ABC. ABC News. "How To Be Safe In America." 1993.

ABC. *Donahue.* 1993.

ABC. Good Morning America. "Kids View the Future." 1993.

ABC. *The Home Show.* (Six shows) 1993.

ABC. *20/20.* "Making Him Pay." 1994.

ABC. *Good Morning America.* "Child Abduction." 1994.

CBS. *48 Hours.* "Missing Without a Trace." 1993.

CBS. *48 Hours.* "Child Hunter." 1994.

Channel 5. *Spectrum.* 1993.

CNN. *Daybreak.* "Two Girls in New Jersey Claim Sexual Abuse by Sex Ring." 1993.

CNN. *Larry King Live.* "The National Crisis of Child Abductions." 1993.

CNN. *Morning News.* "Mother Tries to Make Sense of Daughter's Killing." 1993.

CNN. *Newsnight.* "Chicago Woman Reunited With Seven-Week Old Daughter." 1993.

CNN. *Prime News.* "Southern California Authorities Search for Child Abuser." 1993.

CNN. *Prime News.* "Father Dedicates His Life to Searching for Missing Kids." 1993.

CNN. *Sonya Live.* "Stolen By Strangers." 1993.

CNN. *The World Today.* "Ernie Allen Interviewed About Child Protection Act." 1993.

CNN. *The World Today.* "Parents Express Fear for Their Children's Safety." 1993.

CNN. *The World Today.* "President Clinton Signs Child Protection Act Into Law." 1993.

CNN. *Morning News.* "Dad Lobbies For Polly Klaas Bill Against Repeat Felons." 1994.

CNN. *Morning News.* "Mothers Discuss Their Search for Their Missing Children." 1994.

CNN. *Newsday.* "Linda Ellerbee Teaches Kids How to Respond to Strangers." 1994.

CNN. *Newshour.* "McMartin Molestation Case Leaves Legacy for Preschools." 1994.

CNN. *The World Today.* "Neighborhood Up in Arms With Police Over Child Killer." 1994.

FOX. *America's Most Wanted.* 1993.

HBO. "How to Raise a Street Smart Kid."

NBC. *The Oprah Winfrey Show.* (Two shows) 1993.

NBC. *The Crusaders.* 1994.

NBC. *NOW with Tom Brokaw and Katie Couric.* 1994.

NBC. *Today Show.* 1994.

PBS. "Street Smarts: Straight Talk for Kids, Teens, & Parents." 1992.

Viacom International. *Montel Williams.* "Can You Rehabilitate a Child Molester?" 1994.

WKRC, Cincinnati, Ohio, *Kids and Strangers.*

Radio Programs

NPR. *All Things Considered.* "Chicago Tribune' Series Reports Murders of Children." 1993.

NPR. *Morning Edition.* "Canada Passes Tough Anti-Child Pornography Bill." 1993.

NPR. *All Things Considered.* "Boston Parents Protecting Children From Kidnapping." 1994.

Note: This Bibliography represents the majority of the research sources for this book; however, it is not necessarily a complete listing.

Providing Child Security in Your Community

Yello Dino's products are also available through SAFE-T-CHILD, an international child security and identification organization that has reached over one million children. The SAFE-T-CHILD Program was founded in 1987 to help prevent lost, missing, abducted, and abused children. The Program includes vital educational information for parent and child, memory-enhancing music for children, the invaluable Immediate Response Child I.D. Card, and the new, patented DNA I.D.™ Kit. Certified Directors offer this invaluable Program through schools, daycares, churches, civic organizations, and businesses.

Your Kids are Safe With SAFE-T-CHILD

SAFE-T-CHILD Directors must be service-oriented and have a genuine love for children. Directors include law enforcement officers, ministers, retired military personnel, investigators, school teachers, business men and women, and many other service-oriented people. SAFE-T-CHILD strictly controls the activities of its Directors to ensure not only the quality of the Program, but the privacy and security of the organizations that sponsor the Program, and the parents and children who benefit. SAFE-T-CHILD Directors have the highest level background check that district, county, state, federal, provincial, and/or government laws will allow. The SAFE-T-CHILD Program requires that no records on children are kept by the home office or your local Directors. The Program has been designed to be completely private and confidential.

For More Information About SAFE-T-CHILD

If you would like to see The SAFE-T-CHILD Program offered in your community, check your local white or yellow page listings for your local chapter or call the International Headquarters at (512) 288-2882.

If you would be interested in opening a SAFE-T-CHILD Service Business in your community, please contact the International Headquarters at (512) 288-2882 for detailed information and available territories. SAFE-T-CHILD is a unique and emotionally rewarding investment. If you love children and serving your community, this may be the perfect opportunity. (Average investment: $20,000 U.S.)